elevate science

SAVVAS
LEARNING COMPANY

You are an author!

This is your book to keep. Write and draw in it! Record your data and discoveries in it! You are an author of this book!

Print your name, school, town, and state below.

My Photo

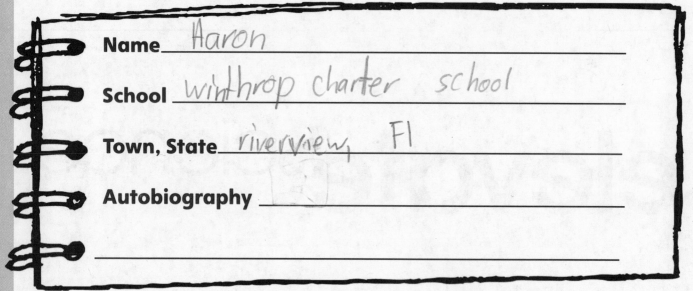

Name Aaron

School winthrop charter school

Town, State riverview, Fl

Autobiography

SAVVAS
LEARNING COMPANY

ISBN-13: 978-0-328-94912-0
ISBN-10:   0-328-94912-4
9 2022

Program Authors

ZIPPORAH MILLER, EdD

Coordinator for K-12 Science Programs, Anne Arundel County Public Schools.
Zipporah Miller currently serves as the Senior Manager for Organizational Learning with the Anne Arundel County Public School System. Prior to that she served as the K-12 Coordinator for science in Anne Arundel County. She conducts national training to science stakeholders on the Next Generation Science Standards. Dr. Miller also served as the Associate Executive Director for Professional Development Programs and conferences at the National Science Teachers Association (NSTA) and served as a reviewer during the development of Next Generation Science Standards. Dr. Miller holds a doctoral degree from University of Maryland College Park, a master's degree in school administration and supervision from Bowie State University, and a bachelor's degree from Chadron State College.

MICHAEL J. PADILLA, PhD

Professor Emeritus, Eugene P. Moore School of Education, Clemson University, Clemson, South Carolina
Michael J. Padilla taught science in middle and secondary schools, has more than 30 years of experience educating middle grades science teachers, and served as one of the writers of the 1996 U.S. National Science Education Standards. In recent years Mike has focused on teaching science to English Language Learners. His extensive leadership experience, serving as Principal Investigator on numerous National Science Foundation and U.S. Department of Education grants, resulted in more than $35 million in funding to improve science education. He served as president of the National Science Teachers Association, the world's largest science teaching organization, in 2005–6.

MICHAEL E. WYSESSION, PhD

Professor of Earth and Planetary Sciences, Washington University, St. Louis, Missouri
An author on more than 100 science and science education publications, Dr. Wysession was awarded the prestigious National Science Foundation Presidential Faculty Fellowship and Packard Foundation Fellowship for his research in geophysics, primarily focused on using seismic tomography to determine the forces driving plate tectonics. Dr. Wysession is also a leader in geoscience literacy and education, including being chair of the Earth Science Literacy Principles, author of several popular geology Great Courses video lecture series, and a lead writer of the Next Generation Science Standards*.

Program Consultants

Carol Baker
Science Curriculum

Dr. Carol K. Baker is superintendent for Lyons Elementary K-8 School District in Lyons, Illinois. Prior to that, she was Director of Curriculum for Science and Music in Oak Lawn, Illinois. Before that she taught Physics and Earth Science for 18 years. In the recent past, Dr. Baker also wrote assessment questions for ACT (EXPLORE and PLAN), was elected president of the Illinois Science Teachers Association from 2011-2013 and served as a member of the Museum of Science and Industry advisory boards in Chicago. She is a writer of the Next Generation Science Standards. Dr. Baker received her BS in Physics and a science teaching certification. She completed her Master of Educational Administration (K-12) and earned her doctorate in Educational Leadership.

Jim Cummins
ELL

Dr. Cummins's research focuses on literacy development in multilingual schools and the role technology plays in learning across the curriculum. *Elevate Science* incorporates research-based principles for integrating language with the teaching of academic content based on Dr. Cummins's work.

Elfrieda Hiebert
Literacy

Dr. Hiebert is the President and CEO of TextProject, a nonprofit aimed at providing open-access resources for instruction of beginning and struggling readers, and a former primary school teacher. She is also a research associate at the University of California Santa Cruz. Her research addresses how fluency, vocabulary, and knowledge can be fostered through appropriate texts, and her contributions have been recognized through awards, such as the Oscar Causey Award for Outstanding Contributions to Reading Research (Literacy Research Association, 2015), Research to Practice Award (American Educational Research Association, 2013), William S. Gray Citation of Merit Award for Outstanding Contributions to Reading Research (International Reading Association, 2008).

Content Reviewers

Alex Blom, Ph.D.
Associate Professor
Department Of Physical Sciences
Alverno College
Milwaukee, Wisconsin

Joy Branlund, Ph.D.
Department of Physical Science
Southwestern Illinois College
Granite City, Illinois

Judy Calhoun
Associate Professor
Physical Sciences
Alverno College
Milwaukee, Wisconsin

Stefan Debbert
Associate Professor of Chemistry
Lawrence University
Appleton, Wisconsin

Diane Doser
Professor
Department of Geological Sciences
University of Texas at El Paso
El Paso, Texas

Rick Duhrkopf, Ph. D.
Department of Biology
Baylor University
Waco, Texas

Jennifer Liang
University Of Minnesota Duluth
Duluth, Minnesota

Heather Mernitz, Ph.D.
Associate Professor of Physical Sciences
Alverno College
Milwaukee, Wisconsin

Joseph McCullough, Ph.D.
Cabrillo College
Aptos, California

Katie M. Nemeth, Ph.D.
Assistant Professor
College of Science and Engineering
University of Minnesota Duluth
Duluth, Minnesota

Maik Pertermann
Department of Geology
Western Wyoming Community College
Rock Springs, Wyoming

Scott Rochette
Department of the Earth Sciences
The College at Brockport
 State University of New York
Brockport, New York

David Schuster
Washington University in St Louis
St. Louis, Missouri

Shannon Stevenson
Department of Biology
University of Minnesota Duluth
Duluth, Minnesota

Paul Stoddard, Ph.D.
Department of Geology and
 Environmental Geosciences
Northern Illinois University
DeKalb, Illinois

Nancy Taylor
American Public University
Charles Town, West Virginia

Safety Reviewers

Douglas Mandt, M.S.
Science Education Consultant
Edgewood, Washington

Juliana Textley, Ph.D.
Author, NSTA books on school
 science safety
Adjunct Professor
Lesley University
Cambridge, Massachusetts

Teacher Reviewers

Jennifer Bennett, M.A.
Memorial Middle School
Tampa, Florida

Sonia Blackstone
Lake County Schools
Howey In the Hills, Florida

Teresa Bode
Roosevelt Elementary
Tampa, Florida

Tyler C. Britt, Ed.S.
Curriculum & Instructional
 Practice Coordinator
Raytown Quality Schools
Raytown, Missouri

A. Colleen Campos
Grandview High School
Aurora, Colorado

Ronald Davis
Riverview Elementary
Riverview, Florida

Coleen Doulk
Challenger School
Spring Hill, Florida

Mary D. Dube
Burnett Middle School
Seffner, Florida

Sandra Galpin
Adams Middle School
Tampa, Florida

Margaret Henry
Lebanon Junior High School
Lebanon, Ohio

Christina Hill
Beth Shields Middle School
Ruskin, Florida

Judy Johnis
Gorden Burnett Middle School
Seffner, Florida

Karen Y. Johnson
Beth Shields Middle School
Ruskin, Florida

Jane Kemp
Lockhart Elementary School
Tampa, Florida

Denise Kuhling
Adams Middle School
Tampa, Florida

Esther Leonard M.Ed. and L.M.T.
Gifted and Talented Implementation Specialist
San Antonio Independent School District
San Antonio, Texas

Kelly Maharaj
Science Department Chairperson
Challenger K8 School of Science and
 Mathematics
Elgin, Florida

Kevin J. Maser, Ed.D.
H. Frank Carey Jr/Sr High School
Franklin Square, New York

Angie L. Matamoros, Ph.D.
ALM Science Consultant
Weston, Florida

Corey Mayle
Brogden Middle School
Durham, North Carolina

Keith McCarthy
George Washington Middle School
Wayne, New Jersey

Yolanda O. Peña
John F. Kennedy Junior High School
West Valley City, Utah

Kathleen M. Poe
Jacksonville Beach Elementary School
Jacksonville Beach, Florida

Wendy Rauld
Monroe Middle School
Tampa, Florida

Anne Rice
Woodland Middle School
Gurnee, Illinois

Pat (Patricia) Shane, Ph.D.
STEM & ELA Education Consultant
Chapel Hill, North Carolina

Diana Shelton
Burnett Middle School
Seffner, Florida

Nakia Sturrup
Jennings Middle School
Seffner, Florida

Melissa Triebwasser
Walden Lake Elementary
Plant City, Florida

Michele Bubley Wiehagen
Science Coach
Miles Elementary School
Tampa, Florida

Pauline Wilcox
Instructional Science Coach
Fox Chapel Middle School
Spring Hill, Florida

Topic 1

Earth's Surface and Weather

SC.2.E.6.1, SC.2.E.6.2, SC.2.E.6.3, SC.2.E.7.1, SC.2.E.7.2, SC.2.E.7.3, SC.2.E.7.4, SC.2.E.7.5, SC.2.P.8.5

▶ VIDEO

📖 eTEXT

👆 INTERACTIVITY

▶ SCIENCE SONG

🎮 GAME

📄 DOCUMENT

✅ ASSESSMENT

Quest

In this Quest activity, you meet a soil scientist. She needs your help to explain how a certain kind of soil came to be near school. You will complete activities and labs. You will use what you learn in the lessons to tell what happens to soil.

Find your Quest activities on pages 11, 17, 25, 32, 38, and 44.

Career Connection Soil Scientist on page 47

The Essential Question

HANDS-ON LAB

Topic 2

Properties of Matter

SC.2.P.8.1, SC.2.P.8.2, SC.2.P.8.3, SC.2.P.8.4, SC.2.P.8.6

 VIDEO

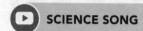 eTEXT

 INTERACTIVITY

 SCIENCE SONG

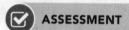 GAME

DOCUMENT

ASSESSMENT

Quest

In this Quest activity, you meet a toy engineer. She needs your help. She wants you to choose materials for a toy kit that kids will use to make model buildings.

Like the toy engineer, you will complete activities and labs. You will use what you learn in the lessons to choose materials for a model building kit. Then you can try to make the kit.

Find your Quest activities on pages 65, 73, 78, and 86

Career Connection Toy Engineer on page 89

The Essential Question

HANDS-ON LAB

Topic 3

Changing Matter

Quest

In this Quest activity, you meet a structural engineer. She is building a bridge. She wants you to help her choose the best materials for the bridge.

Like the structural engineer, you will complete activities and labs. You will use what you learn in the lessons to choose materials for a bridge. Then you will explain your choices in a letter.

Find your Quest activities on pages 107, 113, and 118

Career Connection Engineer on page 123

SC.2.P.8.5, SC.2.P.9.1

- ▶ VIDEO
- 📖 eTEXT
- 👆 INTERACTIVITY
- ▶ SCIENCE SONG
- 🎮 GAME
- 📄 DOCUMENT
- ☑ ASSESSMENT

The Essential Question

HANDS-ON LAB

Topic 4

Energy, Force, and Motion

SC.2.P.10.1, SC.2.P.13.1, SC.2.P.13.2, SC.2.P.13.3, SC.2.P.13.4

 VIDEO

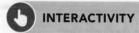 eTEXT

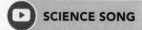 INTERACTIVITY

 SCIENCE SONG

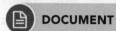 GAME

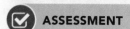 DOCUMENT

ASSESSMENT

Quest

In this **STEM** Quest activity, you meet a civil engineer. He needs your help to design an obstacle course for the school playground. You will complete activities and labs. You will use what you learn in the lessons to design obstacles. Then you will draw your course.

Find your Quest activities on pages 141, 147, 153, 158, and 166

Career Connection Civil Engineer on page 171

The Essential Question

HANDS-ON LAB

SC.2.L.14.1, SC.2.L.16.1, SC.2.L.17.1

Plants and Animals

 VIDEO

 eTEXT

 INTERACTIVITY

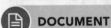 SCIENCE SONG

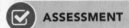 GAME

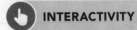 DOCUMENT

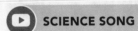 ASSESSMENT

Quest

In this Quest activity, you meet a biologist. He needs help taking care of the plants and animals at a wildlife sanctuary. He would like you to make a healthcare plan for one of the plants or animals.

Like the biologist, you will complete activities and labs. You will use what you learn in the lessons to make a healthcare guide for a plant, for an animal, or for you!

Find your Quest activities on pages 191, 196, 202, and 209

Career Connection Biologist on page 213

The Essential Question

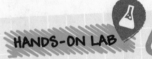

HANDS-ON LAB

Habitats

Quest

In this Quest activity, you meet an ecologist. He would like you to help him make a presentation to city officials. He wants you to explain why the city needs to protect a local habitat.

Like the ecologist, you will complete activities and labs. You will use what you learn in the lessons to make a presentation about a habitat.

Find your Quest activities on pages 230, 239, and 246

Career Connection Ecologist on page 249

▶ VIDEO

📖 eTEXT

👆 INTERACTIVITY

▶ SCIENCE SONG

🎮 GAME

📄 DOCUMENT

☑ ASSESSMENT

HANDS-ON LAB

Elevate your thinking!

Elevate Science for Florida takes science to a whole new level and lets you take ownership of your learning. Explore science in the world around you. Investigate how things work. Think critically and solve problems! *Elevate Science* helps you think like a scientist, so you're ready for a world of discoveries.

Explore Your World

Explore real-life scenarios with engaging Quests that dig into science topics in Florida and around the world. You can:

- Solve real-world problems
- Apply skills and knowledge
- Communicate solutions

Make Connections

Elevate Science connects science to other subjects and shows you how to better understand the world through:

- Mathematics
- Reading and Writing
- Literacy

Quest Kickoff

Find the Parents

What clues help us find a young animal's parent?

Literacy ▸ Toolbox

Main Ideas and Details All living things grow and change is the main idea. Use the details to tell how a watermelon plant changes during its life cycle. LAFS.1.RI.1.2

Math ▸ Toolbox

Compare Numbers You can compare how long objects are. Parent rabbits have longer ears than young rabbits. Use cubes to measure the lengths of two classroom objects. Which is longer? MAFS.1.MD.1.1

Connecting Concepts ▸ Toolbox

Patterns Nature has many patterns. A **pattern** is something that repeats. Parents protect their young. They use their bodies to protect them. What patterns do you see on these two pages?

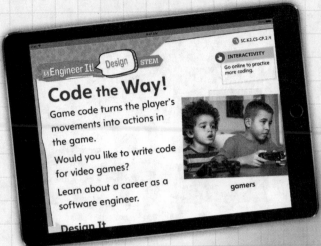

Build Skills for the Future

- Master the Engineering Design Process
- Apply critical thinking and analytical skills
- Learn about STEM careers

Focus on Reading Skills

Elevate Science creates ongoing reading connections to help you develop the reading skills you need to succeed. Features include:

- Leveled Readers
- Literacy Connection Features
- Reading Checks

Literacy Connection

LAFS.1.RI.1.2

GAME
Practice what you learn with the Toolbox Games.

Main Idea and Details

Nature scientists observe animals. Read about the main idea and details of geese and their young.

The main idea is what the sentences are about. Details tell about the main idea.

Enter the Lab Zone

Hands-on experiments and virtual labs help you test ideas and show what you know in performance-based assessments. Scaffolded labs include:

- STEM Labs
- Design Your Own
- Open-ended Labs

Explore the Next Generation Sunshine State Science Standards for:

- Connecting Concepts to make connections
- Nature of Science standards to build inquiry skills
- Big Ideas, Benchmarks, and standards to master content

STEM µInvestigate Lab
HANDS-ON LAB

How do nests protect eggs?

Parent birds build nests. Nests protect the eggs.

Design and Build

☐ 1. Circle the materials you will use to build your nest.

☐ 2. Design your nest. Build it.

☐ 3. Place marbles in your nest.

Evaluate Your Design

Materials
- 1-inch marbles
- nest materials (paper, newspaper, leaves, small paper bags, grass, twigs, modeling clay)

Engineering Practice
You plan a design before you build

Engineering Practice
You plan a design before you build something.

⚠️ **Wash your hands when you are done.**

Earth's Surface and Weather

SC.2.E.6.1 Recognize that Earth is made up of rocks. Rocks come in many sizes and shapes. **SC.2.E.6.2** Describe how small pieces of rock and dead plant and animal parts can be the basis of soil and explain the process by which soil is formed. **SC.2.E.6.3** Classify soil types based on color, texture (size of particles), the ability to retain water, and the ability to support the growth of plants. **SC.2.E.7.1** Compare and describe changing patterns in nature that repeat themselves, such as weather conditions including temperature and precipitation, day to day and season to season. **SC.2.E.7.2** Investigate by observing and measuring, that the Sun's energy directly and indirectly warms the water, land, and air. **SC.2.E.7.3** Investigate, observe and describe how water left in an open container disappears (evaporates), but water in a closed container does not disappear (evaporate). **SC.2.E.7.4** Investigate that air is all around us and that moving air is wind. **SC.2.E.7.5** State the importance of preparing for severe weather, lightning, and other weather related events. **SC.2.P.8.5** Measure and compare temperatures taken every day at the same time. (Also **SC.2.N.1.1, SC.2.N.1.2, SC.2.N.1.5, SC.2.N.1.6, LAFS.K12.R.1.1** and **LAFS.2.RI.2.5, LAFS.2.RI.1.1, MAFS.K12.MP.5.1,** and **MAFS.K12.MP.6.1**)

Go online to access your digital course.

 VIDEO

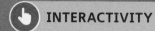 eTEXT

 INTERACTIVITY

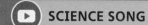 SCIENCE SONG

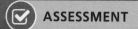 GAME

 ASSESSMENT

The Essential Question

How can weather changes affect different types of soil?

Show What You Know

How do you think weather might change the sand in the picture?

Quest Kickoff

Be a Soil Detective

Where did this soil come from?

Hi! I am Ms. Miller! I am a soil scientist. I study soils. I need your help.

Students have been talking about some "mystery soil." They found the soil near school. It is different from other soil in the area. How did it form? Where did it come from? How did it end up here? You will develop a story that identifies the mystery soil. You will tell where it came from. The path shows the Quest activities you will complete as you work through the topic. Check off your progress each time you complete an activity with a QUEST CHECK ✓ OFF .

Quest Check-In 1

Lesson 1 ■
Observe how rocks break down.

🌸 **SC.2.E.6.2** Describe how small pieces of rock and dead plant and animal parts can be the basis of soil and explain the process by which soil is formed. **SC.2.E.6.3** Classify soil types based on color, texture (size of particles), the ability to retain water, and the ability to support the growth of plants.

Quest Check-In Lab 4

Lesson 4 ▲
Investigate what sunlight does to soil and sand.

Quest Check-In 5

Lesson 5 ★
Read more about what wind and soil do to rocks. Draw a conclusion about how rocks form and change.

Quest Check-In 3

Lesson 3 ◆
Tell what soil looks like and how it affects plants during different seasons.

Quest Check-In Lab 6

Lesson 6 ⬡
Observe how severe weather affects sand.

Quest Check-In 2

Lesson 2 ●
Classify soils. Identify which soils are good for growing some plants.

Quest Findings

Complete the Quest! Find a fun way to tell and show the journey of the mystery soil.

Which water is hotter?

Earth scientists share their observations and look for things that repeat in measurements they make. They use the same tools. What repeating measurements do you see when you share observations?

Materials
- 2 cups of water at different temperatures
- 2 thermometers

Procedure

☐ 1. Place a thermometer in each cup of water. Wait one minute.

☐ 2. Read the temperature of cup A and cup B. Record your data.

Science Practice

You use a tool to make measurements.

	Temperature
cup A	
cup B	

Analyze and Interpret Data

3. Circle data that show which water is hotter.

4. Compare your data with data from another group. Tell if you see data that repeats.

Draw Conclusions

 GAME

Practice what you learn with the Mini Games.

Scientists study how different rocks form. Read about agatized coral.

When you draw conclusions, you use information in a text to figure out meanings the author does not say.

Agatized Coral

Agatized coral is beautiful. It is the state stone of Florida. It can be white, yellow, or red. It is made from ocean animals. After the animals die their skeletons harden. Over millions of years, the skeletons become stone.

☑️ **Reading Check** Draw Conclusions

What conclusion can you draw about where you might find this stone?

_____

_____

_____

SC.2.E.6.1 Recognize that Earth is made up of rocks. Rocks come in many sizes and shapes. (Also SC.2.N.1.1, LAFS.K12.R.1.1, and LAFS.2.RI.1.1)

Lesson 1

Rocks and Minerals

Vocabulary

rock

mineral

I can recognize that Earth is made of many different kinds of rocks that have different sizes and shapes.

Jumpstart Discovery!

Where do you see rocks? Share your ideas. Draw one of the places you have seen rocks.

HANDS-ON LAB
SC.2.E.6.1, SC.2.N.1.1

How can you classify rocks?

Geologists classify rocks to learn more about how rocks form. How can you look for ways that rocks are the same and different?

Materials
• rocks

Procedure

☐ 1. Observe each rock. Record your observations in a chart.

Rock	Color	Shape	Size
Rock 1	Black & Brown	oval	small
Rock 2	black	circle	medium
Rock 3	Tan	long oval	big
Rock 4	Beig	circle	medium

Science Practice

You **classify** when you sort things that are alike and different.

⚠ **Do not throw rocks.**

⚠ **Wash your hands when you are done.**

☐ 2. **Classify** by sorting the rocks into groups.

Analyze and Interpret Data

3. Compare your observations with observations from another group.
Tell how you can sort the rocks again.

Rocks Everywhere

The surface of Earth is made of rocks and other things such as soil and sand. A **rock** is a hard, solid part of Earth.

Some rocks form when volcanoes send lava flowing from an opening. Lava cools and becomes rock. Other rocks form from layers of sand and mud. The layers pile on top of each other and become hard. Some rocks are deep in the ground. Pressure and heat turn them into other kinds of rocks.

INTERACTIVITY

Complete an activity that explores how rocks are made and where they are found.

lava rock

marble

☑ Reading Check Draw Conclusions

What conclusion can you make about how rocks are made?

Formed

Different Rocks

There are many different kinds of rocks. Some rocks are very hard. Others are soft enough that you can scratch them. Some rocks have layers of different colors. Others are just one color. Some rocks feel smooth. Others feel rough.

Rocks are different shapes and sizes. Some rocks are round. Some rocks are bumpy. Boulders are very big. Pebbles are very small.

Observe Look at the rocks. Tell three ways you could sort them.

sandstone   slate   obsidian

Quest Connection

Tell how rocks and soil help make up Earth.

copper

Minerals

Rocks are made up of minerals.
Minerals are nonliving materials that
come from Earth. People use minerals
to make things. For example, people
use the minerals gold and silver to
make jewelry. The mineral copper is
used to make wires for electricity to
pass through. People use the mineral
quartz to make glass.

Most rocks are made up of more than
one mineral. Sandstone is made up
mainly of quartz and the mineral
feldspar. Mica and other minerals can
also be found in sandstone.

gold

Identify Underline three different
uses for minerals.

sandstone

Rocks Break Down

Rocks are everywhere on Earth. They are found under the water. They are found on the surface of land. They are found in dirt. Large rocks can break down and become part of dirt!

Contrast Tell how the rocks look different from each other.

Describe Look at the pictures. Tell what you think happened to the rocks.

Soil

SC.2.E.6.2 Describe how small pieces of rock and dead plant and animal parts can be the basis of soil and explain the process by which soil is formed. SC.2.E.6.3 Classify soil types based on color, texture (size of particles), the ability to retain water, and the ability to support the growth of plants. (Also SC.2.N.1.1, LAFS.K12.R.1.1, and LAFS.2.RI.1.1)

Vocabulary

clay

loam

humus

I can classify different kinds of soil by their traits.

I can explain how soil forms.

Jumpstart Discovery!

Observe some soil. How does it look? How does it feel? Talk about the soil with a partner.

Which soil do beans grow best in?

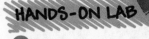

Soil scientists study how well different plants grow in different soils. Which type of soil helps plants grow?

Materials

- 3 plastic cups
- sandy soil
- clay soil
- loam soil
- 6 pinto bean seeds
- water
- graduated cylinder
- tape
- marker
- ruler

Procedure

☐ 1. **Plan an investigation** to determine which soil will best grow seeds. Use all of the materials. Show your plan to your teacher.

☐ 2. Plant the seeds. Observe the seeds for ten days.

Analyze and Interpret Data

3. **Use Evidence** Which soil is better for beans? Use your data to explain why.

_____

_____

_____

4. Tell how you could improve your investigation.

Science Practice

You can **plan an investigation** to answer a question you have about the natural world.

 Wash your hands when you are done.

INTERACTIVITY

Complete an activity on how soil forms.

Soil

Soil is the top layer of Earth. It takes a long time for soil to form. Wind and water wear on rocks. They break rocks into very small pieces. Plants and animals die. They break down into very small pieces. The pieces mix in with the small pieces of rocks.

Soil holds air and water. Rain and snow add water to the soil. Living things also help keep soil healthy. Worms and other animals dig within the soil. This lets in air.

Identify Write in the table three things that are in soil.

Dead leaves become part of soil.

Some Things in Soil

✓ **Reading Check** Draw Conclusions

Tell why it takes a long time for soil to form.

Kinds of Soil

Clay is soil made of small pieces of rock packed together. Clay feels soft, smooth, and sticky. Iron gives some clay its red color. Clay's thick texture holds water well.

Sand is soil made of small, loose pieces of rock. Some sand has a tan color. Sand feels dry and rough. Water runs through it easily.

Loam soil is made of sand, clay, silt, and humus. It has a black color. It can feel moist. Silt is material made of tiny grains of rock. **Humus** is a mix of nutrients from small pieces of dead plants and animals.

Identify Circle words that describe the colors and textures of soils.

clay soil

loam soil

sandy soil

Plants and Soil

It is important for farmers to use the best soil. Without it, they could not grow as much food for others.

Some plants grow well in clay. Clay holds lots of water. Cranberry bushes grow well in clay.

Some plants grow well in sandy soil. Some oak trees grow well in sandy soil. Many plants do not grow well in sandy soil. There is not enough water or nutrients for them.

Most plants grow well in loam. Loam has enough water and nutrients for them.

Classify Circle each type of soil. Underline text that describes the soil by how well it holds water.

plant in clay soil

Quest Connection

Tell why different plants grow best in different soils.

Plants Grow in Soil

Plants need certain things to grow. Corn needs nutrients from living things that have died. Rice needs lots of water. Potatoes need less water. Most plants grow best in the kind of soil that has what they need.

Identify Think of which soil each plant would grow best in. Draw a line from the plant to the soil.

corn

rice

potatoes

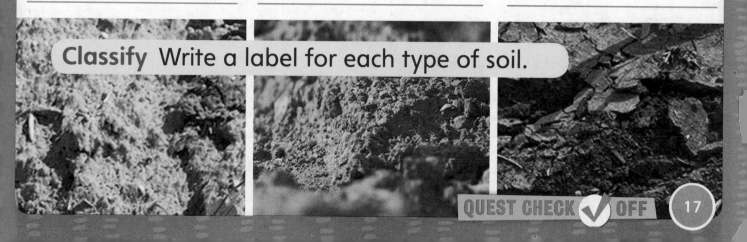

Classify Write a label for each type of soil.

uEngineer It! Improve STEM

INTERACTIVITY

Go online to learn about improving soil.

Improve Plantable Pots

Have you ever seen a pot you can plant? The pots are often made of peat. Peat is a soil-like material. It is partly made of dead plant material. You can plant the pot right in soil. They can cost less money to make. They also break apart over time. They will not become litter.

A gardener uses plantable pots to plant vegetables in his garden. How could you improve these pots? What materials could make up the pot? How might the materials affect the soil when the pot breaks apart? Can your improved pot hold water?

Improve It

☐ List possible ways to improve the design of a plantable pot.

Improvement	How It Improves

☐ Choose one solution from your list. You may combine two solutions. Draw your improved design.

☐ Describe how pieces of your improved plantable pot can become part of soil.

Lesson 3

Changes in Weather

SC.2.E.7.1 Compare and describe changing patterns in nature that repeat themselves, such as weather conditions including temperature and precipitation, day to day and season to season. SC.2.P.8.5 Measure and compare temperatures taken every day at the same time. (Also SC.2.N.1.2, LAFS.K12.R.1.1, LAFS.2.RI.1.1, MAFS.K12.MP.5.1, and MAFS.K12.MP.6.1)

Vocabulary

pattern
temperature
season
precipitation

I can describe how weather conditions follow patterns.

Jumpstart Discovery!

Draw your favorite season.
Tell why it is your favorite.

HANDS-ON LAB

SC.2.E.7.1, SC.2.P.8.5, SC.2.N.1.2

How does weather repeat?

Scientists measure temperature to learn about the weather in a place. They look for things that repeat in their measurements. How can data show you if weather repeats?

Materials

• thermometer

Science Practice

You use a tool to **collect data** by making measurements.

Procedure

☐ 1. Make a plan to measure the daily high and low temperatures. Show your plan to your teacher before you begin.

☐ 2. **Collect data** and record it in the chart.

	Day 1	Day 2	Day 3	Day 4	Day 5
Morning					
Afternoon					

Analyze and Interpret Data

3. **Use data** Tell what you notice about your data. Do you see anything repeat?

4. **Compare** Compare your data with other groups. Talk about what is the same and different.

Math ▸ Toolbox

Use Tools Look at a thermometer carefully when reading it. Make sure you see which marking lines up with the red line. Look at the thermometer in the photo. What temperature does it show?

MAFS.K12.MP.5.1, MAFS.K12.MP.6.1

Weather Patterns

The sun appears to rise in the morning. It appears to set in the evening. This pattern happens every day. A **pattern** is something that repeats. Weather has patterns too. It follows patterns from day to day.

Temperature is how hot or cold something is. In many places, the temperature is cooler in the morning. The temperature is warmer in the afternoon. At night, the temperature is cooler again. This is a pattern of weather.

Predict Draw what you think the thermometer will look like at night.

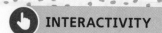

INTERACTIVITY

Complete an activity about the seasons.

Four Seasons

Seasons are a part of the year with different weather patterns. The four seasons of the year are spring, summer, fall, and winter. Different seasons have different weather patterns, including precipitation. **Precipitation** is the water that falls to Earth. You can measure the amount of rainfall with a rain gauge.

rain gauge

Spring and Summer

The temperature can be lower or higher on a spring day. In many places, spring nights are cool. There is a lot of rain in the spring.

In many places, summer days are hot. Summer nights are warm. There is often less rain in the summer than in the spring.

soil in spring

Quest Connection

What do these photos show about soil in spring and summer?

soil in summer

Fall and Winter

Some fall days have high temperatures. Other fall days have lower temperatures. Many nights are cool. Leaves of some trees change color and drop to the ground.

After fall comes winter. Many winter days and nights are cold. In some places, snow falls, and ponds and lakes freeze. Plants do not grow. In Florida, it gets cooler during winter, but not as cold as many other parts of the country. It usually does not snow in Florida.

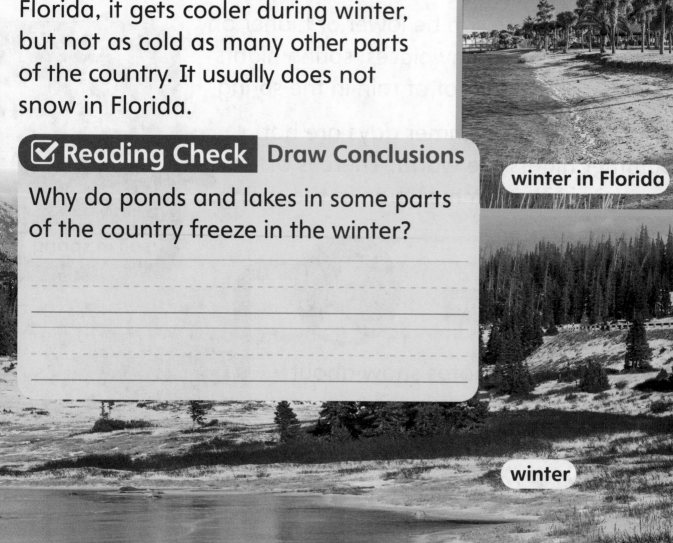

fall

winter in Florida

winter

☑ Reading Check Draw Conclusions

Why do ponds and lakes in some parts of the country freeze in the winter?

_____
_____
_____
_____
_____

Different Seasons, Different Weather

In many places, every season has different weather. Soil can appear different during the seasons.

Describe Tell how weather affects soil in each season.

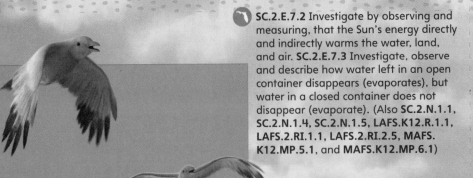

Lesson 4

The Sun

SC.2.E.7.2 Investigate by observing and measuring, that the Sun's energy directly and indirectly warms the water, land, and air. **SC.2.E.7.3** Investigate, observe and describe how water left in an open container disappears (evaporates), but water in a closed container does not disappear (evaporate). (Also **SC.2.N.1.1, SC.2.N.1.4, SC.2.N.1.5, LAFS.K12.R.1.1, LAFS.2.RI.1.1, LAFS.2.RI.2.5, MAFS. K12.MP.5.1,** and **MAFS.K12.MP.6.1**)

Vocabulary

water cycle

water vapor

evaporation

I can investigate how the sun warms the water, land, and air.

I can describe how water evaporates.

Jumpstart Discovery!

Think of activities you do outside in the sunshine. Act one out. Talk about how the sun makes you feel when you are outside.

Where did the water go?

Scientists use models to show things that are hard to see. How can you use a model to show how water disappears from a pond?

Materials

- 2 plastic cups
- 1 plastic lid
- water
- graduated cylinder
- marker

Procedure

☐ **1.** Make a plan to model how the sun affects water. Show your plan to your teacher before you begin. Predict what will happen to the water.

☐ **2.** Set up your model. Make observations.

Science Practice

You can **use a model** to study something in the natural world.

Analyze and Interpret Data

3. Explain How did your observations compare to your prediction?

_____

_____

_____

_____

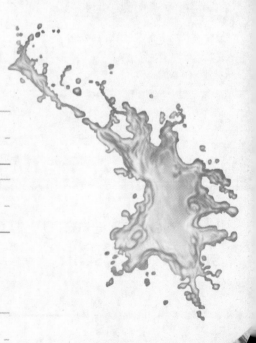

4. Use Models Tell what your model shows about the sun.

_____

_____

Energy from the Sun

Light is one kind of energy. Light energy can make things warmer. Light energy from the sun warms the land, air, and water on Earth.

People visit a beach on a hot day. They notice that the sand is warmer than the water. That is because land heats up faster than water.

Engineering ▶ Toolbox 🔧

Observe Plan an investigation where you can observe the effect of the sun on air and water. Show your plan to your teacher. Follow your plan. Record your observations.

🐊 SC.2.N.1.1

The land _____ the air.

Quest Connection

How does energy from the sun affect soil?

Warm Air

Land and water can also warm air.
Sometimes the water is warmer than the air.
When this happens, the water warms the air.
Sometimes the land is warmer than the air.
When this happens, the land warms the air.

INTERACTIVITY

Complete an activity about how the sun affects temperature.

Identify Study the photo. Compare it to the words on this page. Then write captions for the two blank lines.

The water _____ the air.

Sunlight warms the water.

Sunlight warms the land.

The Water Cycle

Water moves from Earth's surface to the air and back again in the **water cycle**. The sun is the source of energy for the water cycle. The energy of the sun causes liquid water in lakes and oceans to change into water vapor. **Water vapor** is the gas form of water. This process of a liquid changing into a gas is called **evaporation**.

Visual Literacy

Look at the big circle in the picture. Tell why the water cycle does not have a beginning or end.

Connecting Concepts
▶ Toolbox

Patterns The water cycle is a pattern. In the pattern of the water cycle, what comes after precipitation falls to Earth?

SC.2.N.1.1, LAFS.2.RI.2.5

Water vapor turns back to liquid water.

The water evaporates.

Precipitation falls.

Some water sinks into the soil. Some water flows into lakes and oceans.

The sun heats the water.

How does the sun affect loam and sand?

When the sun shines, it warms up land. It is time to investigate how different types of soil are affected by the sun. How can you measure which type of soil warms up to the higher temperature? How might the temperature of the mystery soil give a clue about its journey?

Materials

- 2 plastic cups
- sand
- loam
- 2 thermometers
- stopwatch

Science Practice

Scientists **repeat investigations** to look for patterns in their conclusions.

Procedure

1. Predict which soil will warm more in the sun.

   _____

   _____

2. Plan an investigation to test your prediction. Use all of the materials. Show your plan to your teacher before you begin.

3. Record your observations. Repeat the investigation for two more days.

⚠️ **Wash your hands after touching soil.**

Observations

Soil	Temperature Day 1	Temperature Day 2	Temperature Day 3
Sand			
Loam			

Analyze and Interpret Data

4. **Compare Data** Circle the warmer soil. How does your data compare to your prediction?

_____

_ _ _ _ _ _ _ _ _ _ _ _ _ _ _ _ _

_____

_ _ _ _ _ _ _ _ _ _ _ _ _ _ _ _ _

5. **Analyze** Why is repeating an investigation important?

_____

_ _ _ _ _ _ _ _ _ _ _ _ _ _ _ _ _

_____

Air

SC.2.E.7.4 Investigate that air is all around us and that moving air is wind. (Also SC.2.N.1.1 and SC.2.N.1.5)

Vocabulary

pollution

wind

I can investigate that air is all around us.

I can recognize that moving air is called wind.

Jumpstart Discovery!

Blow on a pinwheel. See what air makes the pinwheel do. Then look out the window. Tell what the moving air outside is making other objects do.

How can a building survive *strong winds?*

Engineers design buildings that can stand up to strong winds. How can you design a model to test if a building will hold up in strong winds?

Suggested Materials

- spoon
- safety goggles
- loam
- sand
- rocks
- container
- paper
- cardboard
- pipe cleaners
- glue
- tape
- scissors
- table fan

Design and Build

☐ 1. List what makes a strong building. Choose materials to make a building.

☐ 2. **Design a model** of your building. Build it.

☐ 3. Use the table fan to test how your building will stand up to strong winds.

Evaluate Your Design

4. Based on your observations, how could you make your building stronger?

_____

_____

_____

_____

Engineering Practice

You design a model to test the solution to a problem.

⚠ Handle scissors with care.

⚠ Do not put your fingers close to the fan.

⚠ Wash your hands when you are done.

Air

Air fills the space between Earth's surface and outer space. Air is made up of gases such as oxygen. Air is all around us even though it cannot be seen.

Pollution is a material that causes harm. It can be found in air. Burning oil, coal, and gasoline can cause pollution.

INTERACTIVITY

Complete an activity about air and wind.

Engineering Practice ▸ Toolbox

Compare Solutions
Think of a solution to help limit pollution. Your solution should help make the air clean. Compare your solution with a classmate.

SC.2.N.1.1

Identify Underline the sentence that describes where air is.

Wind and Its Effects

Wind is moving air. Wind moves in patterns around Earth. You can use tools to measure wind. A wind vane shows which direction the wind blows. An anemometer measures the speed of wind.

anemometer

Wind causes many effects. Wind moves soil from one place to another. It shapes rocks. It shapes sand dunes. Dangerous storms like hurricanes and tornadoes have strong winds. Wind turbines change the wind's energy into electricity.

Explain Tell why the flag is waving. Use the definition of wind.

wind vane

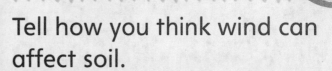

Quest Connection

Tell how you think wind can affect soil.

Wind and Soil Work Together

Goblin Valley State Park in Utah is a fun place to visit. Wind blows soil against the sandstone rocks. This has happened for millions of years. The wind and soil wear away the rocks. They have carved the rocks into interesting shapes.

Illustrate Draw on the rocks. Show what you think they will look like in the future. Show what their size and shape will be.

EXTREME SCIENCE

SC.2.E.7.4, SC.2.E.7.5, LAFS.2.RI.2.5

Hurricane Andrew

Hurricanes are dangerous storms. They have very strong winds. It is important to prepare for a hurricane. You want to stay safe and protect property.

Hurricane Andrew formed in August of 1992. It hit the Bahamas, Florida, and Louisiana. Hurricane Andrew was a Category 5 storm when it reached Florida.

Saffir-Simpson Hurricane Wind Scale

Read the table Circle the wind speed in Hurricane Andrew when it reached Florida.

Category	Wind Speed (m/s)
1	33–42
2	43–49
3	50–58
4	59–69
5	(70 or higher)

Extreme Science 39

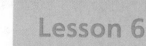

Lesson 6

Stay Safe in Severe Weather

SC.2.E.7.5 State the importance of preparing for severe weather, lightning, and other weather related events. (Also SC.2.N.1.1, LAFS. K12.R.1.1, and LAFS.2.RI.1.1)

I can describe how to stay safe in severe weather.

Vocabulary

severe weather

thunderstorm

tornado

hurricane

Jumpstart Discovery!

Draw a picture of a storm that happened near your house. Talk about the storm. How did you stay safe during the storm?

uInvestigate Lab

How does air move *in a storm?*

Scientists study air and the way it moves. How can you use a model to understand how air can move in a storm?

Materials
- round container
- water
- straw

Procedure

☐ 1. In some storms, air moves in circles. How can you model the way air moves? Use the materials.

☐ 2. Plan a **model**. Build and use it.

☐ 3. Record your observations.

Science Practice

Scientists use models to study the natural world.

Observations

Analyze and Interpret Data

4. What happened in the container? How does air move in a storm?

_____

_____

_____

Thunderstorms and Tornadoes

Severe weather is dangerous weather. It is important to stay safe during severe weather. **Thunderstorms** have strong winds, heavy rains, thunder, and lightning.

A **tornado** is a column of wind shaped like a funnel. Tornadoes come down from thunderstorm clouds. Tornadoes form very quickly. They are hard to predict. A tornado can destroy things in its path.

☑ Reading Check Draw Conclusions

Tell why it is important to prepare for tornadoes and other severe weather.

⚠ Thunderstorm and Tornado Safety

- Stay away from water and trees.
- For thunderstorms, stay away from metal objects. Stay away from things that use electricity.
- For tornadoes, go to the basement or an inside room.
- Find shelter inside a sturdy building. Stay away from windows.

Connecting Concepts ▸ Toolbox 🔧

Patterns When one kind of weather happens, another kind of weather usually happens. What weather usually happens before a tornado?

tornado

Hurricanes

Hurricanes are another kind of severe weather. A **hurricane** is a large storm that starts over warm ocean water. A hurricane has heavy rains. The rains can cause floods. A hurricane has very strong winds. The winds can knock down trees and buildings. Hurricanes sometimes strike Florida.

Describe Circle where a hurricane starts. Underline words that describe weather during a hurricane.

INTERACTIVITY

Complete an activity about staying safe in severe weather.

⚠ **Hurricane Safety**

- Move away from the ocean.
- Bring loose objects inside.
- Stay inside. Stay away from windows.
- Store extra food and water in your home.

hurricane

Quest Connection

Tell what a hurricane could do to Earth's surface and soil.

What happens to a sand dune *during a storm?*

Scientists investigate the effect of severe weather on sand dunes. Think of how severe weather may have caused sand to become part of the mystery soil. How can you observe what happens to a sand dune in a storm?

Suggested Materials

- table fan
- sand
- newspaper
- measuring tape
- container
- tray
- stopwatch
- water
- safety goggles

Science Practice

You **observe** when you look closely at things.

⚠ Do not put your fingers close to the fan.

⚠ Wash your hands when you are done.

⚠ Wear safety goggles when investigating.

Procedure

☐ 1. Think of a way to model the effect of severe weather on sand dunes. Draw a picture of what you will do on a piece of paper. Show your teacher.

2. Set up your model. **Observe** what happens to the sand. Repeat three times. Record your data.

Observations

Trial	
1	
2	
3	

Analyze and Interpret Data

3. Analyze How could severe weather impact what is in the mystery soil?

_____

_____

4. Explain How could the movement of sand during severe weather be dangerous?

_____

_____

Quest Findings

 INTERACTIVITY

Apply what you learned in the Quest.

Be a Soil Detective

Where did this soil come from?

Show What You Found

Remember the mystery soil that students found near the school. What could have happened to the soil before it was found? How did it form? Where did it come from?

Now it is time for you to tell the story of the soil. You can write a story, draw a poster, or make a video about the soil's journey. Be creative! Show how many things can happen to soil.

QUEST CHECK ✓ OFF

Soil Scientist

Soil scientists study soil. They test the soil. They identify kinds of soil in an area.

They tell farmers how to improve soil. This helps plants grow. Some soil scientists study how soils can support buildings. Some investigate how soils affect the water cycle. Others find out how to stop wind and water from moving soil.

What would you study if you were a soil scientist?

_____

_ _ _ _ _ _ _ _ _ _ _ _ _ _ _ _ _ _

_____

_ _ _ _ _ _ _ _ _ _ _ _ _ _ _ _ _ _

_____

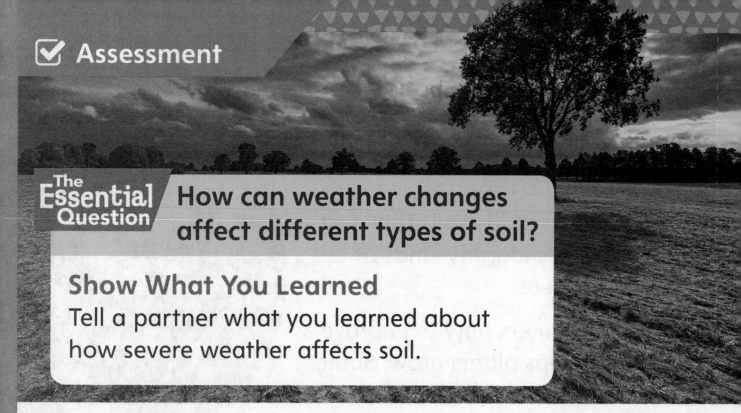

| The Essential Question | How can weather changes affect different types of soil? |

Show What You Learned
Tell a partner what you learned about how severe weather affects soil.

Read each question and choose or write the best answer.

1. Ted wanted to find out how winter is different in Florida compared to other states. Which information would NOT help him make this comparison?

State	Number of Winter Days	Ice Formation on Lakes	Lowest Temperature	Number of Snowy Days
Florida				
Illinois				
Colorado				
Vermont				

   a. Number of winter days
   b. Ice formation on lakes
   c. Lowest temperature
   d. Number of snowy days

2. Describe two actions a person should take to be safe during a hurricane.

_____

- -

_____

- -

3. Write what the wind does to the soil and rocks in the photo.

Soil -

_____

Rocks -

4. Describe what happens when a puddle of rain evaporates.

_____

- -

_____

- -

_____

Read the scenario and answer questions 1–2.

A scientist tested soil types. She filled three cups with different soils. She added water to each cup until the soils were soaked.

The table shows the mass of soil before and after the water was added.

Soil Type	Mass of soil in cup	Mass of soil and water in cup	Soil Color
1	40 g	45 g	light brown
2	30 g	40 g	red
3	30 g	50 g	dark brown

1 What does the evidence tell you about Soil Type 3?

Ⓒ It can hold more water than the other soil types.

Ⓓ It is the same type of soil as Soil Type 1.

Ⓔ It is probably the soil type called sand.

Ⓕ It is dark brown because it is the heaviest.

2 Based on the evidence, which soil type is most likely sand?

Ⓕ Type 1 because it is light brown in color.

Ⓖ Type 3 because it has the most water in it.

Ⓗ Type 1 because its final mass is the lowest.

Ⓘ Type 3 because its final mass is the greatest.

Read the scenario and answer questions 3–4.

Eli's graph shows patterns of evaporation.

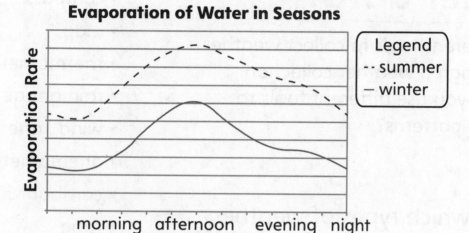

Evaporation of Water in Seasons

Legend
-- summer
— winter

Evaporation Rate

morning   afternoon   evening   night
Time of Day

3 Which pattern is described by the evidence?

Ⓐ More water vapor forms in the night than in the afternoon.

Ⓑ Less water vapor forms in the morning than in the afternoon.

Ⓒ More sunlight in the summer causes less water vapor to form.

Ⓓ Less sunlight in the winter causes more water vapor to form.

4 Where do you think a line for spring would be on the graph?

Ⓕ above the line for summer

Ⓖ between the lines for summer and winter

Ⓗ under the line for winter

Ⓘ on the same line as summer

How can I collect weather data?

Scientists use different tools to collect weather data. You will design a weather collection station. How can you use different tools to measure weather patterns?

Procedure

1. Choose which types of weather you want to measure. Your station should collect data on at least three of these: temperature, precipitation, wind direction, and wind speed.

2. Draw a design for your weather collection station.

Suggested Materials

- modeling clay
- compass
- map
- thermometer
- rain gauge
- wind vane
- anemometer
- cardboard
- tape
- glue
- scissors

Science Practice

You **use a tool** to make measurements.

3. Choose materials to build your station. Build it. Add the tools to it.

4. Plan when and where to measure the weather. Show your plan to your teacher. Collect the data. Record the data in a table.

Day 1	Day 2	Day 3

Analyze and Interpret Data

5. What patterns do you see in the data you collected?

_____

_____

_____

_____

6. Compare your data with data collected by another group. How are your observations on weather patterns the same or different?

_____

_____

_____

_____

Properties of Matter

SC.2.P.8.1 Observe and measure objects in terms of their properties, including size, shape, color, temperature, weight, texture, sinking or floating in water, and attraction and repulsion of magnets. **SC.2.P.8.2** Identify objects and materials as solid, liquid, or gas. **SC.2.P.8.3** Recognize that solids have a definite shape and that liquids and gases take the shape of their container. **SC.2.P.8.4** Observe and describe water in its solid, liquid, and gaseous states. **SC.2.P.8.6** Measure and compare the volume of liquids using containers of various shapes and sizes. (Also **SC.2.N.1.1, SC.2.N.1.3, SC.2.N.1.5, SC.2.N.1.6, LAFS.K12.R.1.1, LAFS.2.RI.1.1, LAFS.2.RI.1.3, MAFS.2.MD.1.1, MAFS.K12.MP.5.1,** and **MAFS.K12.MP.6.1**)

▶ VIDEO

📖 eTEXT

👆 INTERACTIVITY

▶ SCIENCE SONG

🎮 GAME

☑ ASSESSMENT

The Essential Question   How can different materials be used?

Show What You Know

Look at the picture. How can the materials be used?

Toy Building Kit

Why do we use different materials for a toy kit?

Hi! I am Dr. Ayashi. I am a toy engineer. I study materials to make toys. I also test toys. I want them to be safe. I want them to last a long time.

I need to design a kit for kids to make model buildings. Help me pick objects for the kit. Observe and test objects. Keep track of your observations in a chart. The path shows the Quest activities you will complete. Check off your progress each time you complete an activity with a **QUEST CHECK ✓ OFF**.

Quest Check-In 1

Lesson 1 ■

Use what you learned to classify objects as solid, liquid, or gas. Decide if the objects are good for building.

SC.2.P.8.1 Observe and measure objects in terms of their properties, including size, shape, color, temperature, weight, texture, sinking or floating in water, and attraction and repulsion of magnets. (Also **SC.2.N.1.1, SC.2.N.1.5,** and **SC.2.N.1.6**)

Quest Check-In Lab 3

Lesson 3 ◆

Use what you learned about the properties of blocks to build something.

VIDEO

Watch a video about a toy engineer.

Quest Check-In 2

Lesson 2 ●

Use what you learned about properties of matter. Observe and classify building blocks.

Quest Check-In 4

Lesson 4 ▲

Use what you learned about liquids and gases. Explain if you could use liquids and gases in the kit.

Quest Findings

Complete the Quest! Use your chart. Describe what materials you would include in the toy building kit.

Which object is **bigger?**

Engineers observe the materials they use. They also measure them. How do you know one object is bigger than another?

Materials
- two objects

Suggested Materials
- ruler
- connecting blocks
- paperclips

Procedure

☐ **1.** Look at two objects. Think of how you can show which is bigger. Make a plan to investigate.

☐ **2.** Measure the objects. **Collect data.**

Science Practice

You measure to collect data.

Observations	

Analyze and Interpret Data

3. Circle data that show which object is bigger. Underline data that show which object is smaller.

4. Tell how you know which object is bigger.

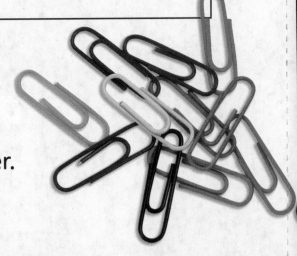

LAFS.K12.R.1.1, LAFS.2.RI.1.1, LAFS.2.RI.1.3

Cause and Effect

An engineer may need to test materials. One test could include magnets. Read about the causes and effects of using magnets on different materials.

A cause makes something happen. An effect is the result.

GAME

Practice what you learn with the Mini Games.

Magnets

You want to test if materials are magnetic. Materials are magnetic if they are able to be pushed or pulled by a magnet. You place a magnet on the back of a plastic chair. The magnet does not stick. Next, you put the magnet on the metal leg of the chair. The magnet sticks to the leg of the chair! The metal leg is magnetic. The plastic seat is not.

☑ **Reading Check** Cause and Effect

Underline what causes a magnet to stick. Circle the effect that plastic has on a magnet.

plastic chair with metal legs

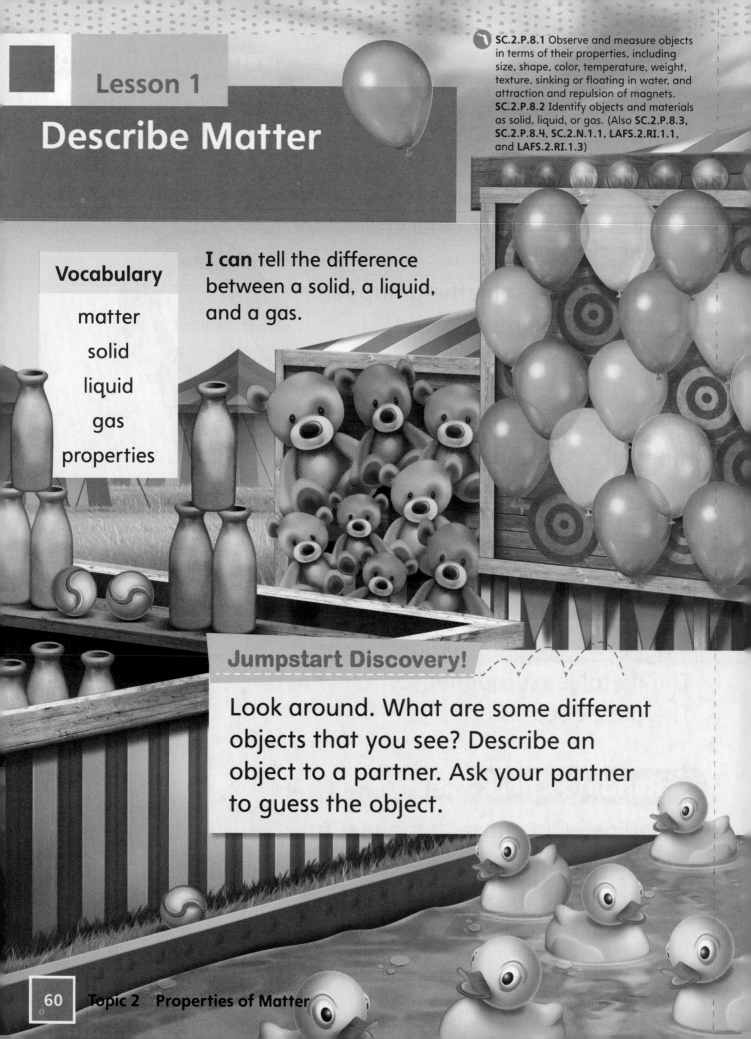

SC.2.P.8.1 Observe and measure objects in terms of their properties, including size, shape, color, temperature, weight, texture, sinking or floating in water, and attraction and repulsion of magnets. SC.2.P.8.2 Identify objects and materials as solid, liquid, or gas. (Also SC.2.P.8.3, SC.2.P.8.4, SC.2.N.1.1, LAFS.2.RI.1.1, and LAFS.2.RI.1.3)

Lesson 1

Describe Matter

Vocabulary

matter

solid

liquid

gas

properties

I can tell the difference between a solid, a liquid, and a gas.

Jumpstart Discovery!

Look around. What are some different objects that you see? Describe an object to a partner. Ask your partner to guess the object.

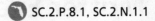
What is different?

Life scientists sort plants and animals based on their features. How can you sort objects?

Procedure

☐ **1. Observe** six objects.

☐ **2.** Sort the objects at least three different ways. Use the features of the objects to help you decide.

Analyze and Interpret Data

3. How did you sort the objects?

_____

_____

_____

_____

4. How did another group sort differently?

_____

_____

_____

_____

Suggested Materials

- cup
- book
- eraser
- calculator
- ball
- water
- magnet
- letters

Science Practice

You **observe** when you look closely at things.

Matter Everywhere

Look around you. Everything you can see, touch, or smell is made up of matter. **Matter** is anything that has weight and takes up space. A desk is made of matter. A chair is made of matter. Everything is made up of matter even if you cannot tell it is there.

paint

To describe matter, you observe its properties. **Properties** are the traits or features of an object. Color, shape, and size are properties.

Identify Circle matter that is blue.

Explain How do you know if something is matter?

Types of Matter

↻ **INTERACTIVITY**

Complete an activity on classifying matter.

A **solid** is matter that has its own size and shape. A **liquid** is matter that does not have its own shape. A **gas** is matter that does not have its own shape or size. Liquids and gases take the shape of their containers.

The balls are all solid. Some are made of rubber, plastic, or fabric. Some of the balls are filled with air. Air is made of gases.

soccer ball

tennis ball

> **Observe** Look at the balls in the pictures. Circle the largest ball. Place an X on the smallest ball.

football

> ☑ **Reading Check** Cause and Effect
> A ball is being filled with air. Tell what you think the effect is on the ball's shape.

basketball

Describe Matter

Some properties you can observe with your senses. You can measure other properties.

Think about liquid water and frozen water. Water is a liquid. An ice cube is frozen water. It is a solid. The ice cube is cold. Liquid water can be cool, warm, or hot. You can measure their temperatures.

Label each item as a solid, liquid, or gas.

Literacy ▸ Toolbox 🔧

Cause and Effect If you freeze water, what is the effect? What would cause an ice cube to turn back into liquid water?

🐊 LAFS.2.RI.1.1, LAFS.2.RI.1.3

Quest Connection

Could you use ice cubes to build a toy house in a warm room? Why or why not?

Build with Solids, Liquids, and Gases

Some objects do a job better than others. You can observe the properties of an object. You can see if the object would be good for a job.

Object			
Type of Matter			
Properties			
Useful for Building			

Collect Data Classify objects as solid, liquid, or gas. Record your data in the chart. What objects would you put in your kit? Why?

_____

_____

_____

_____

QUEST CHECK ✓ OFF   65

Design a Nutcracker!

Nutcrackers are tools. People use nutcrackers to open the hard shells of nuts.

Some animals also eat nuts. The tools they use can be part of their bodies. Birds use their beaks. Squirrels use teeth to crack nuts. Some animals bang the nut to open it. Some animals drop the nuts from high above to try to break them open.

Look at the pictures of these animals.

ground squirrel

parrot

They eat nuts and hard seeds. What do you notice about their mouths?

Model It

Nutcrackers are usually made from hard, strong materials. They must be easy to hold. They must be hard enough to crack a nut. How can you make a nutcracker by modeling after the animals?

☐ Draw a design of your model nutcracker.

☐ Label the materials used in each part of the nutcracker.

☐ Share your design. Compare it to another design.

☐ Tell how you could improve your design.

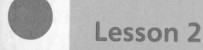
Properties of Matter

SC.2.P.8.1 Observe and measure objects in terms of their properties, including size, shape, color, temperature, weight, texture, sinking or floating in water, and attraction and repulsion of magnets. (Also **SC.2.P.8.3**, **SC.2.N.1.1**, **SC.2.N.1.6**, and **LAFS.2.RI.1.3**)

I can describe matter by its properties.

Vocabulary

weight

texture

magnetic

flexibility

hardness

Jumpstart Discovery!

Look at the dam. What slows down the flow of the water? Discuss with a partner.

What can beavers teach **engineers?**

Engineers can learn from nature. Beavers build dams to change the flow of water. Engineers also build dams. How can you change the way water flows?

Materials
- plastic bin
- water

Suggested Materials
- craft sticks
- glue
- modeling clay
- pipe cleaners

Design and Build

- ☐ 1. **Make a model** dam that stops water. Choose your materials.
- ☐ 2. Design your dam. Build it in the plastic bin.
- ☐ 3. Test it by adding water to one side of it.

Engineering Practice

You **make a model** to show how something works.

Evaluate Your Design

4. How well did your dam hold water?

_____

- - - - - - - - - - - - - - - - - -

_____

5. Compare your dam to others in the class. Tell which properties of matter are good for building a dam.

Measure Properties

Many properties can be measured. Scientists measure accurately. For example, you can measure temperature and weight. **Weight** is how heavy an object is.

▶ **VIDEO**

Watch a video about properties of matter.

measuring oranges

farmers' market

Observe Properties

You can observe the size, color, and shape of an object. Texture is another property. **Texture** is how something feels. An object may feel soft, smooth, rough, or bumpy. You can see some textures.

Visual Literacy Look at the picture. Use properties of matter to describe what you see.

Contrast Tell how the textures of the fruits and vegetables are different.

Test Properties

Some metals are magnetic. An object that can be pushed or pulled by a magnet is **magnetic.**

You can test if an object will sink or float. An object can float if it has air inside of it or if it is light and has a large surface.

INTERACTIVITY

Complete an activity on identifying properties of matter.

☑ **Reading Check** Cause and Effect Underline what causes an object to float.

You may also need to test for flexibility. Matter that has **flexibility** is able to bend. If an object can scratch another object, then it is harder than that object. **Hardness** is a property that tells how hard or solid an object is compared to other objects.

objects sinking and floating

Quest Connection

Is flexibility a property of a building block? Why or why not?

Observe, Measure, Test

Some properties you can observe. Others you may need to measure or test.

Look at the images of the blocks. Which properties can you observe?

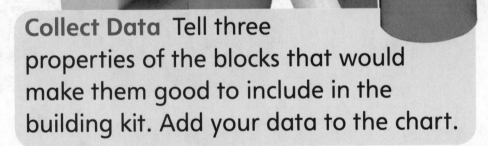

Collect Data Tell three properties of the blocks that would make them good to include in the building kit. Add your data to the chart.

Measure and Test Properties of Blocks	
Properties	**How to Measure or Test Properties**

Lesson 3
Use Solids

SC.2.P.8.2 Identify objects and materials as solid, liquid, or gas. SC.2.P.8.3 Recognize that solids have a definite shape and that liquids and gases take the shape of their container. (Also SC.2.P.8.1, SC.2.N.1.3, SC.2.N.1.6, LAFS.2.RI.1.1, LAFS.2.RI.1.3, and MAFS.2.MD.1.1)

Vocabulary

purpose

I can investigate how the properties of some solids make them useful.

Jumpstart Discovery!

Think of a solid object you use at home. Act out using the object. Do not speak. Have a partner guess what the object is. What clues did your partner use?

Which package fits the blocks?

Engineers learn about the properties of a material to know how to use it. What properties of a solid can you use to help you decide which package to use?

Materials

- ten building blocks
- small and large cardboard boxes
- small and large plastic bags

Procedure

☐ 1. **Observe** the size and shape of the ten blocks together.

☐ 2. Predict which container will fit all the blocks. Predict whether the blocks will change shape when moved into a container.

☐ 3. Test your prediction.

Science Practice

You **observe** when you look closely at things.

Analyze and Interpret Data

4. Which containers best fit the blocks?

_____

_____

_____

5. How do you know the blocks are solid?

_____

_____

_____

Uses of Solids

▶ VIDEO
Watch a video about using solids.

When building a house, each material has a purpose. A **purpose** is the use of an object. Wood makes the frame of the walls and roof. Bricks might be used to keep out wind, heat, or cold air. If you use brick for the roof it might fall down! You can measure the materials to decide how much you need.

☑ **Reading Check** Cause and Effect Underline the effect that heavy bricks could have on the roof of a house.

Everyday Solids

People use solids every day. You use a solid cup when you drink. You use a solid plate when you eat. You play with solid toys.

Solids come in many shapes and sizes. They can be different materials. They can be glass, metal, plastic, or concrete. Sometimes solids are made of more than one material.

Identify Tell what materials are used in this house. Why are the materials good for their job?

INTERACTIVITY

Complete an activity on building with solids.

Math ▸ Toolbox

Measuring Objects
Tell two ways you can measure a solid like your chair or desk. Measure one of these objects. Compare your results with a classmate.

MAFS.2.MD.1.1

Quest Connection

What solids would you include in your toy building kit?

How do you use shapes when building?

Materials
• building blocks of different sizes and shapes

It is time to design a solution for building with shapes. We need to make a plan and choose the right materials. What materials will we use in the kit?

Engineering Practice

Engineers **design a solution** to a problem or question by making a plan and choosing the right materials.

Design and Build

☐ **1.** Identify which blocks might be good for building a house. Describe them in the chart.

☐ **2.** **Design a solution** for what you will build with the blocks.

☐ **3.** Think of two other structures someone might want to build with toy blocks. Write them in the chart.

☐ **4.** Build the structures. Keep track of the blocks you used.

Item	Blocks Used
House	

Evaluate Your Design

5. How did you choose the materials for your design solution?

_____

_____

_____

6. What was the purpose of different blocks?

_____

_____

_____

_____

Use Liquids and Gases

SC.2.P.8.2 Identify objects and materials as solid, liquid, or gas. SC.2.P.8.3 Recognize that solids have a definite shape and that liquids and gases take the shape of their container. SC.2.P.8.6 Measure and compare the volume of liquids using containers of various shapes and sizes. (Also SC.2.P.8.1, SC.2.P.8.4, SC.2.N.1.5, LAFS.2.RI.1.1, LAFS.2.RI.1.3, MAFS.K12.MP.5.1, and MAFS.K12.MP.6.1)

Vocabulary

state

I can investigate how the properties of some liquids and gases make them useful.

Jumpstart Discovery!

Think about gas in the form of wind, your breath, and the air around us. Draw a picture that shows different ways we use gases.

How can you make a bigger **bubble?**

Materials

- water
- liquid soap
- bubble wands
- graduated cylinder
- 3 plastic cups

Scientists study liquids and gases. How does the amount of soap compared to water affect the size of a bubble?

Procedure

☐ 1. What do you know about bubbles? Predict if more or less soap will produce a bigger bubble.

☐ 2. Make a plan to test your prediction. Use all of the materials.

☐ 3. Show your plan to your teacher. Run your test. **Collect data**.

Science Practice

Scientists **collect data** when they investigate a question.

Observations			
Test Number	Amount of water	Amount of Soap	Results
1			
2			
3			

Analyze and Interpret Data

4. Tell if your observations supported your prediction.

Shapes of Liquids and Gases

Liquids and gases do not have a shape. They take the shape of their container. Their shape changes if their container changes.

> ☑ **Reading Check** Cause and Effect What determines the shape of a liquid?
>
> _____
>
> _____

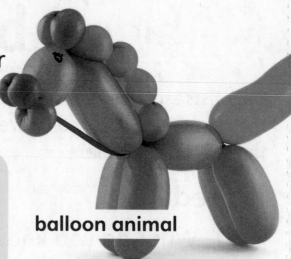

balloon animal

The air in your classroom is made of gases. It takes the shape of your classroom. Air inside bicycle tires is the same shape as the tires. Look at the balloon animal. It is filled with gas.

balloons

Quest Connection

Can you use liquid or gas to build a house? Why or why not?

States of Matter

You know that water can be liquid or solid. Water can also be a gas. Water that is a gas is called water vapor. You cannot see water vapor. Solid, liquid, and gas are states of matter. A **state** of matter is a form of a matter.

Identify Underline the three different states of water. Circle the name of the gas state of water.

melting wax crayons

wax crayons

VIDEO

Watch a video about using liquids and gases.

Connecting Concepts ▸ Toolbox

Constructing Explanations Why do you think we use gas instead of liquid inside balls and tires? SC.2.N.1.5

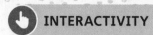
Measure Liquids

You can measure how much space a liquid or gas takes up.

You can measure liquids using containers. Pour a liquid into a container. The liquid will always take up the same amount of space. Measuring instruments make measuring liquids easy.

Identify Underline what happens to liquid when you pour it into a container.

Observe Tell which container has the most amount of water.

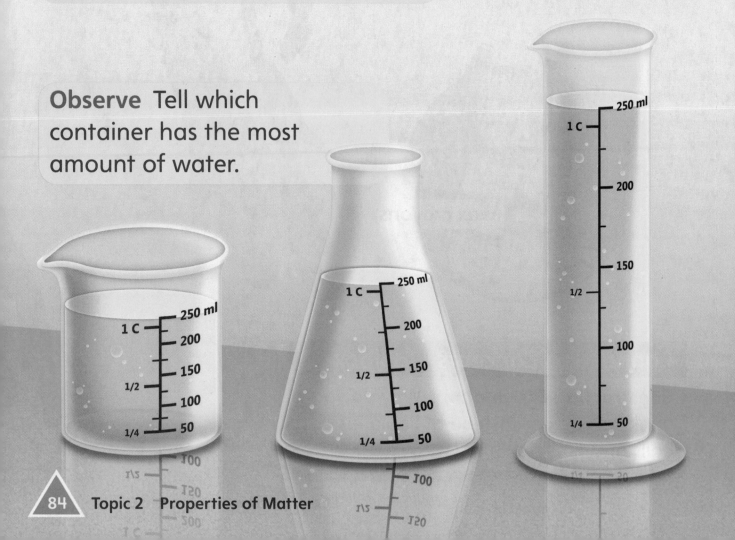

Everyday Uses of Liquids and Gases

There is liquid in the food we eat. We drink water. We also cook and wash with water. Your body is made mostly of water! Water helps you move and stay warm. Another important liquid is gasoline. We use gasoline in cars to get around. Trucks, ships, and planes use gasoline to deliver things we need.

food delivery truck

Identify Circle one way you use a liquid.

Air contains different gases. Oxygen is a gas in air. You need it to breathe. Many homes use natural gas for heating and cooking. If you see a flame in your oven or on a stove, then your home uses natural gas.

stove with natural gas

Identify Underline one way you use a gas.

Liquid and Gas Toys

You are almost ready to make the toy building kit. You have tested different solids. Now think about other states of matter. Be creative!

Explain What are some ways you could use liquids and gases in the kit?

_____

- - - - - - - - - - - - - - - - - - -

_____

- - - - - - - - - - - - - - - - - - -

_____

SC.2.P.8.1, MAFS.K12.MP.5.1,
MAFS.K12.MP.6.1

Measure Temperature

A thermometer measures temperature.
There are many different kinds of
thermometers. Some are digital. Some
use a liquid called alcohol inside the
thermometer. As the temperature rises,
alcohol expands, or gets bigger. The
alcohol rises inside the thermometer as the
temperature rises.

Read the temperature on
each thermometer. Write the
temperatures in the boxes.

INTERACTIVITY

Apply what you learned in the Quest.

Toy Building Kit

Why do we use different materials for a toy kit?

Look back at your chart. Choose the best materials for the kit to make model buildings.

Show What You Found

Identify which materials go into the kit. You can make a list of the objects. You can also draw them. Try making the kit. Remember to include any packing materials. What are some similarities of the objects in the kit? What are some differences? What properties of objects make them good for building?

QUEST CHECK ✓ OFF

Toy Engineer

Toy engineers make toys. They often work on a team. It is their job to make a toy the best it can be. They test toys to make sure they are safe. They make toys easier to build. They pick the best materials to use for a type of toy. Some use computers to design or test toys. Others work in the toy factory.

Toy engineers pay attention to materials. They observe properties of the materials to make the toy better.

Why is this an important job?

_____

- -

_____

- -

_____

_____

The Essential Question

How can different materials be used?

Show What You Learned

Tell a partner how you can use a solid, a liquid, and a gas for certain jobs.

Read each question and choose or write the best answer.

1. How would you describe the properties of this ball?
   a. large, smooth, blue
   b. small, bumpy, green
   c. large, bumpy, orange
   d. small, soft, orange

2. Hoda wants a box that is see-through and easy to carry. Which kind of material do you recommend the box be made of?
   a. glass
   b. metal
   c. plastic
   d. wood

3. Which property is most likely **measured** when describing a solid object?

   a. texture
   b. color
   c. flexibility
   d. weight

4. Look at the picture. Circle one example of a liquid. Put an X on a gas. Draw a box around a solid.

Read the scenario and answer questions 1–2.

Mary investigated the property of objects. The picture shows her investigation.

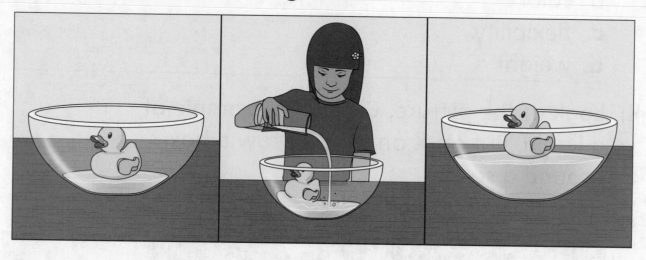

1 Which of the following is NOT a property of the toy duck?

Ⓐ It is liquid.

Ⓑ It can float.

Ⓒ It has texture.

Ⓓ It has shape.

2 Which property of the water changes as Mary pours it from the glass to the bowl?

Ⓕ color

Ⓖ texture

Ⓗ shape

Ⓘ size

Read the scenario and answer questions 3–4.

Bianca recorded information about four samples of matter.

	Shape	Magnetism	Texture	Color
Sample 1	circle	yes	smooth	red
Sample 2	none	no	cannot tell	green
Sample 3	square	no	rough	black
Sample 4	none	no	cannot tell	no color

3 Which property **best** helps you identify the sample that might be a gas?

Ⓐ shape

Ⓑ magnetism

Ⓒ texture

Ⓓ color

4 Based on the table, which samples could be liquids?

Ⓕ Sample 1 and Sample 2

Ⓖ Sample 2 and Sample 4

Ⓗ Sample 3 and Sample 4

Ⓘ Sample 1 and Sample 3

What makes something sink or float?

Boat engineers collect data about if materials sink or float before they build a boat. How can you collect data to tell which objects sink or float?

Procedure

☐ 1. Choose and observe four objects. Predict if each one will sink or float.

☐ 2. Make a plan to test each object. Show your plan to your teacher.

☐ 3. Run your test. **Collect data** in the table.

Materials

• bin
• water

Suggested Materials

• paperclips
• corks
• erasers
• craft sticks
• foil sheets
• small balloons
• clay

Science Practice

Scientists **collect data** when they investigate a question.

Observations

Object	Observed Properties	Sink or Float?

Analyze and Interpret Data

4. **Explain** Why do some objects float and why do some objects sink?

_____

_____

_____

5. **Predict** Decide if one of the objects you did not test will sink or float. How do you know whether it will sink or float?

_____

_____

_____

_____

Topic 3

Changing Matter

SC.2.P.8.5 Measure and compare temperatures taken every day at the same time. **SC.2.P.9.1** Investigate that materials can be altered to change some of their properties, but not all materials respond the same way to any one alteration. (Also **SC.2.N.1.1, SC.2.N.1.3, LAFS.K12.R.1.1, LAFS.2.RI.1.1, LAFS.2.RI.1.3, MAFS.2.MD.4,** and **MAFS.K12.MP.6.1**)

Go online to access
your digital course.

▶ VIDEO

📖 eTEXT

👆 INTERACTIVITY

▶ SCIENCE SONG

🎮 GAME

☑ ASSESSMENT

The Essential Question

How do you change materials?

Show What You Know

Look at the photo. Tell how the ice is changing.

Building Bridges

What are the best materials to use in building a bridge?

Hi! My name is Ms. Kuan. I am an engineer. I am working at a construction site. We are building some tall buildings. We need to build a bridge. It will connect different areas of the site.

The bridge needs to be strong. It will carry people and trucks. The bridge will be used in summer and winter. Sometimes it will be used in high winds. Help me find the best materials we should use to build the best bridge for this job. The path shows the Quest activities you will complete as you work through the topic. Check off your progress each time you complete an activity with a **QUEST CHECK** **OFF** .

Quest Check-In 1

Lesson 1 ■ ○

Use what you learned to identify changes to matter.

🌀 **SC.2.P.8.5** Measure and compare temperatures taken every day at the same time. **SC.2.P.9.1** Investigate that materials can be altered to change some of their properties, but not all materials respond the same way to any one alteration. **SC.2.P.9.In.1** Explore and identify that observable properties of materials can be changed. **SC.2.P.9.Su.1** Recognize changes in observable properties of materials. **SC.2.P.9.Pa.1** Recognize that the appearance of an object or material has changed. Also **SC.2.N.1.1, SC.2.N.1.3, SC.2.N.1.5, SC.2.N.1.6, LAFS.K12.R.1.1, LAFS.2.RI.1.1, LAFS.2.RI.1.3, MAFS.K12.MP.5.1,** and **MAFS.K12.MP.6.1)**

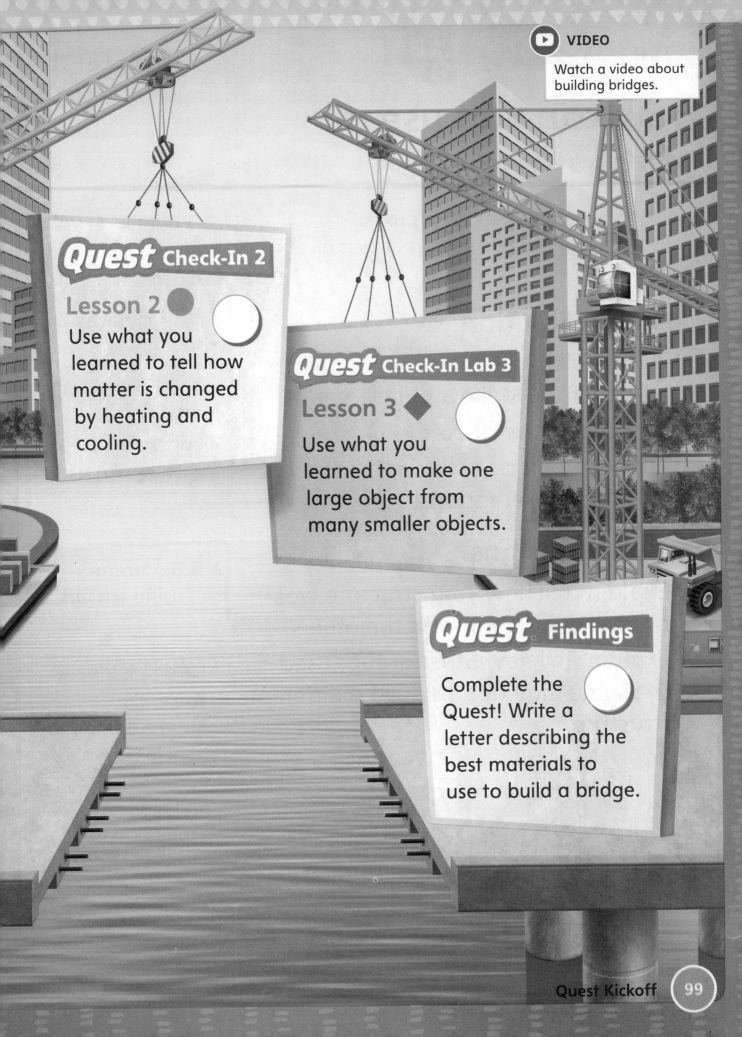

VIDEO

Watch a video about building bridges.

Quest Check-In 2

Lesson 2 ●

Use what you learned to tell how matter is changed by heating and cooling.

Quest Check-In Lab 3

Lesson 3 ◆

Use what you learned to make one large object from many smaller objects.

Quest Findings

Complete the Quest! Write a letter describing the best materials to use to build a bridge.

How can you use all of the materials?

Engineers use a list of materials to build a structure. What can you build that uses all of the materials?

Design a Solution

- [ ] **1.** Use all of the materials to build a structure. Make a plan.
- [ ] **2.** Build your structure.
- [ ] **3.** Trade objects with another group. **Make observations.**

Evaluate Designs

4. **Explain** Tell how your structure was alike and different from the others.

5. **Explain** Tell how other groups used the same materials to build a different structure.

Materials

- cardboard tubes
- pieces of cardboard
- craft sticks
- toothpicks
- glue
- tape
- paper clips
- scissors

⚠ **Be careful using scissors.**

Engineering Practice

You **make observations** to help collect evidence and make explanations.

Sequence

Scientists need to follow steps in a **sequence** to do a job. Sequence means to put steps in order.

GAME

Practice what you learn with the Mini Games.

A Cool Snack

Here is a recipe to make frozen juice pops. First, get some fruit. Next, have an adult cut the fruit into small pieces. Then, put the fruit pieces into the blender. Watch as the blender turns the fruit into juice. Pour the juice into an ice cube tray. Finally, put the ice cube tray into the freezer. After 4-6 hours, you will have frozen juice pops.

☑ Reading Check **Sequence** Underline the sentence with the word *First*. Draw a circle around something that happens next. Draw a square around the thing that happens last.

Why is it important to follow a sequence in a recipe?

_____

_____

Observe Changes in Matter

SC.2.P.9.1 Investigate that materials can be altered to change some of their properties, but not all materials respond the same way to any one alteration.

SC.2.N.1.1 Raise questions about the natural world, investigate them in teams through free exploration and systematic observations, and generate appropriate explanations based on those explorations.

Vocabulary

matter

I can explore different ways matter can change.

Jumpstart Discovery!

Hold a piece of paper. Change the paper. Can you undo the change?

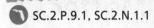
How can you *change* objects?

Scientists observe how objects can be changed. How many ways can you change something?

Procedure

☐ **1.** Use the materials. Make a plan to make at least three changes.

☐ **2.** Show your teacher your plan.

☐ **3.** Follow your plan. Make observations.

Materials

- clay
- 3 to 5 drops of food coloring
- plastic gloves

 ⚠ **Wear plastic gloves.**

Science Practice

You **construct explanations** when you use evidence from your observations.

Analyze and Interpret Data

4. Explain Tell if you made changes that could be undone. What were they?

5. Explain Tell if you made changes that could not be undone. What were they?

▶ VIDEO

Watch a video about changing matter.

Matter Can Change

Think about the sidewalk at school. The sidewalk is made of matter. **Matter** is anything that takes up space. The sidewalk is a solid, but it is made up of three types of matter including liquid water.

Here is how to build a sidewalk. First, you need three ingredients: water, sand, and cement. Next, mix the sand and cement together. Then, slowly add the water until the mixture is almost too hard to stir. Now, these ingredients are called concrete. Finally, your concrete is ready to pour to make your sidewalk.

☑ **Reading Check** Sequence

Underline the first thing you need to do to make a sidewalk.

Quest Connection

Tell how the materials you use to build a bridge will decide what properties it has.

You Can Change Matter

Sometimes you can change the features of matter. You can change solid matter by cutting, bending, and folding it. You can change matter by tearing, taking it apart, and breaking it. You take a ball of clay. You make an animal shape. You change the features of the clay. You can change the clay back to its original shape.

Large machines are used to mix and pour concrete to make a sidewalk.

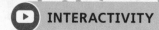
Matter Changes in Many Ways

You can make orange juice from fresh oranges. You change the solid fruit into a liquid. You cannot change the orange juice back into oranges though! Matter does not always change in the exact same way. Sometimes you can undo the change you made. Sometimes you cannot.

You make a change in matter. The object you changed looks different from its original shape or form. A flat piece of paper can be used for writing or coloring. If you make a paper animal, the paper looks completely different. The paper animal also has a different purpose. You play with the animal, you don't write on it.

Matter Can Change

Look at the photos. Each photo shows how matter can change. Sometimes you can change the matter back to what it used to be. Sometimes you cannot.

Interactivity Circle the changes you can undo. Put an X on the changes you can't undo.

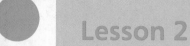

Lesson 2

Temperature and Matter

SC.2.P.8.5 Measure and compare temperatures taken every day at the same time. SC.2.P.9.1 Investigate that materials can be altered to change some of their properties, but not all materials respond the same way to any one alteration. SC.2.N.1.3 Ask 'how do you know?' in appropriate situations and attempt reasonable answers when asked the same question by others. (Also MAFS.2.MD.4)

Vocabulary

property

reversible

I can explain whether a change caused by heating or cooling matter is reversible.

I can explain whether a change caused by heating or cooling matter is not reversible.

Jumpstart Discovery!

What is happening to the crayons? Act it out.

uInvestigate Lab

How does heating and cooling change matter?

Scientists learn how matter changes when it is heated or cooled. What observations can you make about the claim that heating or cooling changes matter?

Materials

- crayons
- freezer
- heat source
- thermometer
- ice cube trays
- metal spoon
- oven mitt

Procedure

☐ **1.** Make a plan to add heat to the crayon and to chill the crayon.

☐ **2.** Show your plan to your teacher before you start.

☐ **3.** Record your results.

Science Practice

You **use evidence** to support a claim.

⚠ **Do not touch heat source.**

⚠ **Wear gloves when handling hot or cold objects.**

Analyze and Interpret Data

4. Explain Tell if you could make the crayon look exactly the way it did when you started.

Temperature

You can observe the properties of matter. A **property** is something about an object you can observe with your senses. Temperature is a property of matter. How hot or cold is it outside? You can measure this

property of matter with a thermometer. A thermometer is a tool that measures how hot or cold it is.

The days of the week are in a sequence that repeats week after week, every year. For one week, take the temperature outside at exactly the same time every day. Record your observations in the chart. How did the temperature change each day?

Monday	Tuesday	Wednesday	Thursday	Friday
Sunshine	Rain	Clouds	Sunny	Sunny
26 °C (80 °F)	20 °C (68 °F)	22 °C (72 °F)	25 °C (77 °F)	28 °C (83 °F)

Monday	Tuesday	Wednesday	Thursday	Friday

VIDEO

Watch a video about heating and cooling.

Heating and Cooling

The place where polar bears live has both liquid water and solid ice. This place is called the Arctic. The temperatures in the Arctic are very cold. Cold can change matter. In the winter the liquid water freezes. It turns to solid ice. Some of the ice stays in its solid shape year round.

In the summer the temperatures in the Arctic are warm. Warmth can also change matter. Some of the solid ice that formed in the winter melts. It turns to liquid water. These changes caused by heating and cooling happen over and over again, year after year.

Quest Connection

Tell how temperature changes can help you decide what materials to use to build your bridge.

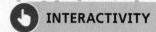
Reversible or Not

Some changes made by heating and cooling can be **reversible**. They can be changed back to the way they were.

Some changes made by heating and cooling cannot be changed. They can never be changed back to the way they were.

Which changes can be reversed? Circle them.

Which changes cannot be reversed? Put an X on them.

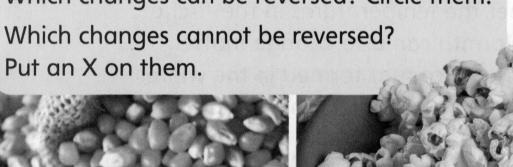

How does temperature change matter over time?

Think about different materials that could be used for a bridge. Some bridges are made of rope. Others might use steel coils or concrete columns. How might the temperature affect each of these materials?

Steel coil

Look at the chart. The chart shows materials that might be good to use to build a bridge. Some materials are a good choice for both cold and warm weather.

Surfaces for Bridges	Properties in Warm Weather	Properties in Cold Weather	Best in All Kinds of Weather
Rope	strong, may be slippery when wet	strong, but could be dangerous in icy weather	
Concrete	strong, and good in warm weather	strong, and good in cold weather	
Wood	strong, may be slippery when wet	strong, but could be dangerous in icy weather	

Identify Which surface has the best properties for both warm and cold weather? Put an X in that row. Tell why.

Lesson 3

Matter Within Objects

▶ **VIDEO**

Watch a video that shows smaller objects being used to build larger objects.

SC.2.P.9.1 Investigate that materials can be altered to change some of their properties, but not all materials respond the same way to any one alteration. **SC.2.N.1.1** Raise questions about the natural world, investigate them in teams through free exploration and systematic observations, and generate appropriate explanations based on those explorations.

Vocabulary

assemble

I can explain that objects can be built using smaller materials.

I can explain that objects are built using materials that have certain properties.

Jumpstart Discovery!

Look at the roller coaster. What is it made of? Think of one word to describe the roller coaster. Tell a partner!

What can you build?

Look at the list of materials. How can you use these objects to build something?

Design a Solution

☐ 1. Think of a problem you want to solve. Choose materials. **Design a Solution.**

☐ 2. Show your plan to your teacher.

☐ 3. Build your solution.

☐ 4. Tell another group how your design works.

Evaluate Your Design

5. Did your solution solve the problem you identified? Why or why not?

_____

_____

_____

_____

6. How can you change your design to make it better?

_____

_____

_____

_____

Suggested Materials

- building blocks
- cardboard
- toothpicks
- craft sticks
- pipe cleaners
- glue
- tape
- clothes pins
- clay
- safety scissors

⚠ Be careful using scissors.

Engineering Practice

You **design a solution** when you plan to build something to solve a problem.

Objects Can Be Assembled from Other Objects

INTERACTIVITY

Learn to take something apart to make something new.

A small model of a real plane has many parts. When you put the parts together, you assemble them to make your model plane. **Assemble** means to put together. There is a sequence you have to follow in order to correctly put something together. Look at the pictures. They are not in the correct order. Show how you can you put a model plane together.

Visual Literacy

Sequence Number the steps to show how you would put the plane together in the proper sequence.

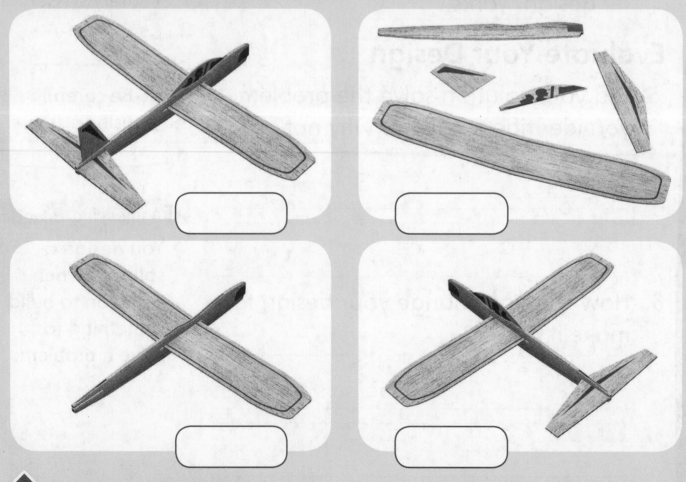

Choose one of the objects shown. Draw a large object made up of many of the small objects. Write a caption for your drawing. Label one of the small objects. Then explain what the purpose was of the object you drew.

Quest Connection

Tell how you can use many small objects to make a large object, such as a bridge.

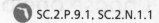
What materials make a bridge strong?

Bridges are used for different purposes in different places. What materials will you use to make your bridge strong?

Suggested Materials

- two desks
- string
- craft sticks
- cardboard
- plastic cups
- straws
- pipe cleaners
- glue

Design and Build

☐ **1. Design a solution.** You need a strong bridge to cross the space between two desks.

☐ **2.** Choose materials to build your bridge.

☐ **3.** Show your plan to your teacher.

☐ **4.** Build your bridge. Record each material you used.

☐ **5.** Test how strong your bridge is by putting blocks on it.

Engineering Practice

Engineers design a solution to a problem by making a plan and choosing the right materials.

Evaluate Your Design

6. Evaluate Tell which materials worked best for your bridge. Explain.

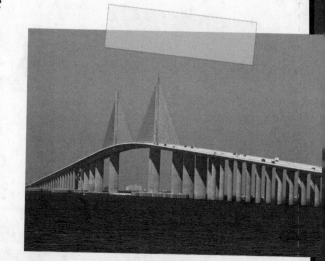

STEM ⟩ Math Connection

MAFS.2.MD.4

Compare Numbers

Scientists use the Celsius scale to measure temperature.

When water freezes, it measures 0 °Celsius (C). It can also be measured as 32 °Fahrenheit (F). The ° symbol means *degrees*.

Look at the thermometers. To tell the temperature you look at the top of the red line and read the numbers on either side of it.

Circle the summer temperature. Put an X on the winter temperature. Write these two temperatures below. How do these numbers compare?

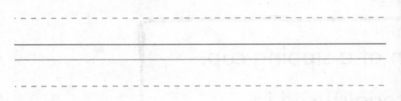

uEngineer It! Improve STEM

Improve a Sipping Cup!

INTERACTIVITY

Go online to learn more about how certain materials are used for specific purposes.

Your baby sister uses a sipping cup to drink her milk. She brings it to her mouth. It leaks all over her. The cup is not supposed to leak. Something is wrong with this cup! Can you tell what the problem is by looking at the picture? Think about how you can stop the cup from leaking.

Improve It

Think about the materials you would need to build a new sipping cup for your sister that doesn't leak. What are the parts of the cup that you will need to assemble a new cup? What will your design be to solve this problem?

- ☐ Draw a design of a sipping cup.
- ☐ Label the materials used in each part of the cup.
- ☐ Share your design. Compare it to another design.

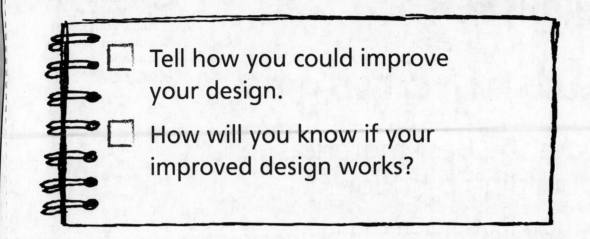

- [ ] Tell how you could improve your design.
- [ ] How will you know if your improved design works?

INTERACTIVITY

Apply your Quest learnings to a new scenario.

Building Bridges

What are the best materials to use in building a bridge?

You saw how matter can change. You saw how hot weather and cold weather could change matter. You built a model bridge. You chose materials to make it strong.

Show What You Found

Write a letter to Ms. Kuan. Explain to her which materials you think she can use to build her bridge. You can make a list of the materials. You can also draw them. Tell Ms. Kuan why you think these materials are the best to use to build a strong bridge in warm and cold weather.

QUEST CHECK ✓ OFF

Structural Engineer

Structural engineers design things you use every day. They design buildings, bridges, tunnels, and homes. They often work together as a team. It is their job to make sure that what they build is safe and strong. They also need to make sure they use the right materials to get the job done. Structural engineers work at construction sites and many other places.

Structural engineers pay attention to materials used to build things. They observe a material's properties to make sure the project does what it needs to do.

Tell why is this an important job.

The Essential Question

How do you change materials?

Show What You Learned
Tell a partner how you can change ice into water.

Read each question and choose or write the best answer.

The pictures shows four different changes in matter.

1
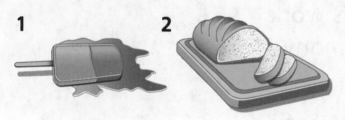

2

3

4

1. Look at pictures 1 and 4. Why did the matter change in both pictures?

_____

_____

_____

2. Why are the changes shown in the pictures NOT reversible?

_____

_____

3. Mariam is building a house out of a large cardboard box. If Mariam uses tape to close the box, what kind of change did she make?

_____

_____

4. Shazia used a thermometer every day for a science project. Which kind of project do you think she was doing?
   a. measuring changes to how hot or cold something is
   b. measuring how long it takes ice cubes to melt into liquid
   c. changing liquid matter into gas matter
   d. changing matter in a way that is reversible

5. Lee built a house. It is shown in the picture. His dog knocked it over. Why can Lee put it back together in the same way?

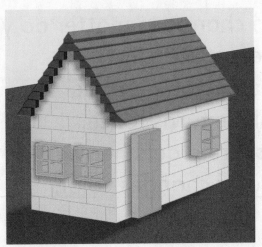

Read the scenario and answer questions 1–2.

A family wanted to go swim at the beach.

Celsius Temperature Chart	
Temperature	**Outdoors**
-20°C	
-10°C	
0°C	ice melts and water freezes
5°C	a cold day in winter
10°C	
15°C	a warm winter day or a cool summer day
20°C	
25°C	
30°C	a hot summer's day
40°C	dangerously hot

1 Which temperature would be **best** for the family to go swimming at the beach?
Ⓐ 15°C
Ⓑ 20°C
Ⓒ 25°C
Ⓓ 35°C

2 Which change in matter do you think could happen at -20°C?
Ⓕ Metal would break.
Ⓖ A lake turns to ice.
Ⓗ Concrete gets heavier.
Ⓘ Water changes color.

Read the scenario and answer questions 3–4.

Amy's diagram shows how different temperatures can change different kinds of matter, such as crayons.

3 What effect did the refrigerator have on the crayons?

Ⓐ made the temperature go up

Ⓑ changed the shape

Ⓒ made the size get bigger

Ⓓ changed the color

4 Which picture could cause a change in the crayons that could not be reversed?

Ⓕ picture 1

Ⓖ picture 2

Ⓗ picture 3

Ⓘ picture 4

5 What **best** explains what happens to a pencil's properties when you sharpen it?

Ⓐ The shape will not change.

Ⓑ It will have more weight.

Ⓒ The temperature will change.

Ⓓ The change cannot be reversed.

How can you make something new?

Materials
• blocks of different sizes and colors

Engineers use the objects they have to make something new. They think about what the object must do. They find the parts they need. They assemble the parts into something new.

Engineering Practice

Engineers make observations to help collect evidence and make explanations.

Design Solutions

☐ **1.** Look at the blocks. Identify a problem you want to solve. Build a structure with all the blocks to solve the problem.

☐ **2.** Draw your structure.

☐ **3.** Identify a second problem you want to solve. Build a new structure with all the same blocks to solve the second problem.

☐ **4.** Draw your new structure.

Analyze and Interpret Data

☐ **5. Explain** how each structure solved a problem.

_____

- -

_____

_____

- -

_____

☐ **6. Explain** how you used the same materials
   to solve two problems.

_____

- -

_____

_____

- -

_____

Energy, Force, and Motion

SC.2.P.10.1 Discuss that people use electricity or other forms of energy to cook their food, cool or warm their homes, and power their cars. **SC.2.P.13.1** Investigate the effect of applying various pushes and pulls on different objects. **SC.2.P.13.2** Demonstrate that magnets can be used to make some things move without touching them. **SC.2.P.13.3** Recognize that objects are pulled toward the ground unless something holds them up. **SC.2.P.13.4** Demonstrate that the greater the force (push or pull) applied to an object, the greater the change in motion of the object. (Also **SC.2.N.1.1, SC.2.N.1.2, SC.2.N.1.3, SC.2.N.1.4, SC.2.N.1.5, SC.2.N.1.6, LAFS.2.RI.3.8, LAFS.K12.R.1.1, MAFS.K12.MP.2.1,** and **MAFS.2.MD.2.5**)

Go online to access
your digital course.

▶ VIDEO

📖 eTEXT

👆 INTERACTIVITY

▶ SCIENCE SONG

🎮 GAME

☑ ASSESSMENT

The Essential Question What are some ways different objects can move?

Show What You Know

Look at the picture. How do you think these cars can move?

STEM Design an Obstacle Course

What forces are at work in an obstacle course?

Hi! I am Mr. Martinez! I am a civil engineer. I plan, design, and build things. I work on roads, bridges, and buildings.

I need your help to design an obstacle course. It is for a school playground. Students will use pushes and pulls to do the obstacles.

As you read, look for details that may help you build the course. The path shows the Quest activities you will complete as you work through the topic. Check off your progress each time you complete an activity with a **QUEST CHECK ✓ OFF**.

Quest Check-In 1

Lesson 1 ■

Identify potential energy and kinetic energy.

SC.2.P.13.1 Investigate the effect of applying various pushes and pulls on different objects. SC.2.P.13.3 Recognize that objects are pulled toward the ground unless something holds them up. SC.2.P.13.4 Demonstrate that the greater the force (push or pull) applied to an object, the greater the change in motion of the object.

▶ VIDEO

Watch a video about a civil engineer.

Quest Check-In 2

Lesson 2 ●

Use what you have learned. Sort actions into pushes or pulls.

Quest Check-In 3

Lesson 3 ◆

Explore what type of obstacle would need a stronger push or pull to complete.

Quest Check-In 4

Lesson 4 ▲

Decide if magnets can be used in an obstacle course.

Quest Check-In Lab 5

Lesson 5 ☆

Investigate the effect of gravity on water. Decide how you could use water in an obstacle course.

Quest Findings

Complete the Quest! Use what you know about energy, force, and motion. Design an obstacle course for a school playground.

What forces are used in tug-of-war?

What happens if two forces are applied to the same object at the same time?

Procedure

☐ 1. Make a plan to apply more than one force to the string. Show your plan to your teacher.

☐ 2. **Investigate** applying the forces to your string. Repeat at least four times. Record your data.

Material
- string

Suggested Material
- stickers

Science Practice

You **repeat scientific investigations** to see how results compare.

Observations

Analyze and Interpret Data

3. **Explain** Tell about the results when you repeated the investigation.

Use Evidence from Text

Scientists can use wind turbines. These machines help make electricity. Read about how we can make electricity from wind.

When you use evidence from text, you find information in the text. The information supports a statement or idea.

Wind Power

Wind turbines are machines. The wind blows. It turns the blades. The machine changes the motion of the blades into electricity. Electricity from wind does not cost much to make. We will never run out of wind. Wind turbines do not cause pollution.

✓**Reading Check** Use Evidence from Text Underline evidence that shows why wind turbines are a good way to make electricity.

Using Energy

VIDEO

Watch a video about uses of energy.

SC.2.P.10.1 Discuss that people use electricity or other forms of energy to cook their food, cool or warm their homes, and power their cars. (Also SC.2.N.1.1, LAFS.2.RI.3.8, and LAFS.K12.R.1.1)

Vocabulary

energy

electricity

kinetic energy

potential energy

I can explain how people use energy in many different ways.

CHARGING STATION

Jumpstart Discovery!

Look at the picture. What do you think helps this car to run?

How can an object change from being (still) to having m o t i o n ?

Suggested Materials
• toy car
• ramp
• ball
• yo-yo

Scientists study how objects move. How can you investigate the start and stop of motion?

Procedure

☐ 1. Decide which materials to use.

☐ 2. Make a plan to investigate how motion starts and stops. Show your plan to your teacher.

☐ 3. Conduct your investigation. **Observe** the motion of the objects.

Science Practice

You make observations to help answer a scientific question.

Analyze and Interpret Data

4. **Explain** How did you change the motion of an object?

_____

_____

_____

_____

Energy

Energy is the ability to do work or cause change. **Electricity** is a kind of energy that moves through wires. It makes light and heat. An air conditioner uses electricity. It cools your home. A furnace can use electricity. It warms your home. Electricity turns on lights.

Heat is the movement of energy from warmer places and objects to cooler ones. Energy moves from the hot burner on the stove. Energy moves to the pot. Then energy moves from the hot pot. The energy moves to the cold food.

INTERACTIVITY

Complete an activity about energy use in homes.

Literacy ▸ Toolbox

Use Evidence from Text Read about how people use energy. People use electricity to change the temperature in their homes. Underline evidence in the text that supports this idea.

LAFS.2.RI.3.8, LAFS.K12.R.1.1

Illustrate Show how energy moves. Draw arrows on the picture.

food cooking on stove

Cars and Energy

Most cars get energy from fuel. Most cars use gasoline as a fuel. The car's engine burns the fuel. This gives the car the energy to move. A car will not move without fuel.

Some cars use electricity to move. People plug their cars into a power source. This charges the car battery. Other cars use biofuels. These are fuels made of things like plants.

Filling a car with gasoline

Identify Circle three different types of energy that cars use to move.

Charging an electric car

☑ **Reading Check** **Use Evidence from Text**
Predict what would happen if a car runs out of gasoline. How do you know? Underline text that supports your idea.

_____

_____

_____

_____

Types of Energy

Kinetic energy is the energy of motion. People use kinetic energy when they walk, run, or jump.

puffin

Potential energy is stored energy related to an object's position. An object has more potential energy the higher it is above the ground.

An object can have both kinetic energy and potential energy at the same time. For example, an object that moves and is high above the ground has both.

Identify Look at the pictures. Draw an X on the bird that has more kinetic energy.

Quest Connection

Tell when people use kinetic energy in an obstacle course.

Quest Check-In

Forms of Energy

People use energy when they run an obstacle course. Dogs also like to run obstacle courses!

Identify Which dog has more potential energy? Which dog uses kinetic energy? Write the correct term under each photo.

_____

_____

Explain A dog has potential energy. Tell how the dog can change to also use kinetic energy.

QUEST CHECK ✓ OFF

141

SC.2.P.13.1 Investigate the effect of applying various pushes and pulls on different objects. (Also **SC.2.N.1.1, SC.2.N.1.3, LAFS.2.RI.3.8,** and **LAFS. K12.R.1.1**)

Motion and Force

Vocabulary

motion

force

I can investigate how forces change the way objects move.

Jumpstart Discovery!

Look at the photo. Describe how objects move when bowling. What other ways can objects move?

How can you make an object that moves?

Engineers study different ways objects move. How can you design and build an object that moves?

Design and Build

☐ 1. Choose the materials you will use. **Draw a design** of your object on a piece of paper.

☐ 2. Make a plan to build your object and test how it moves. Show your plan to your teacher.

☐ 3. Conduct your test.

Evaluate Your Design

4. **Evaluate** How did your design work?

_____

_____

_____

5. **Evaluate** What did you do to get your object to move?

_____

_____

_____

_____

_____

Suggested Materials

- scissors
- cardboard tubes
- cardboard box
- egg cartons
- lids from jars
- bottle tops
- pipe cleaners
- straws
- glue
- string

 Be careful using scissors.

Engineering Practice

You **draw a design** to plan how to build something.

Motion

When something is moving, it is in **motion.** Objects can move in different ways. Suppose you push a toy train. Then you pull it back toward you. The toy train moves in a straight line.

You may move the train in a zigzag motion. This means you push the train one way. Then you push it another way.

Identify Show which way the toy train moves. Draw arrows on the picture. Tell how someone can make the toy train move.

Connecting Concepts ▸ Toolbox

Cause and Effect Look at the picture of the train. How will the shape of the tracks affect the motion of the train?

SC.2.N.1.3

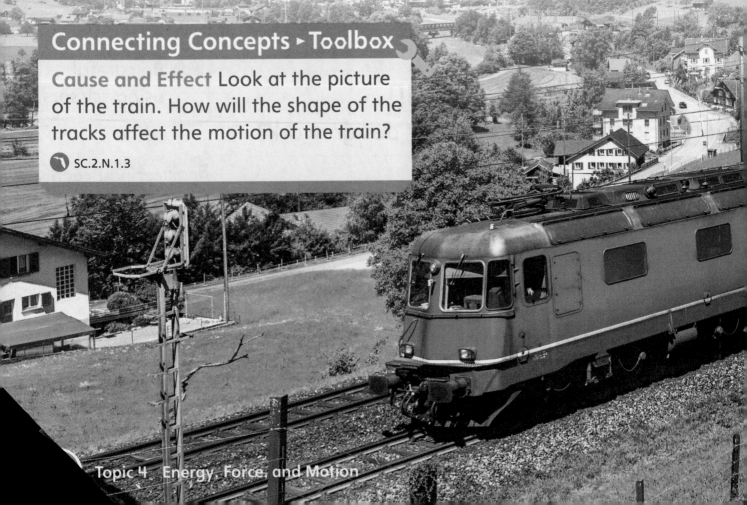

Force

A **force** is a push or a pull that makes something move. A force changes the way an object moves.

You need to use more force to move heavier objects than lighter objects. Suppose you are pushing a toy train with cargo. The train is easier to move when it is empty. The train is harder to move when it is full.

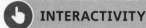
INTERACTIVITY

Complete an activity to investigate motion and force.

full cargo

empty cargo

☑ **Reading Check** Use Evidence from Text

Does a lighter object or a heavier object need more force to move it? Underline the text that supports your conclusion.

Position

Position is where something is located. To tell about your position, look at another object. Where are you in relation to that object?

Think about when you go to bed at night. Your position is on top of the bed. You play hide-and-seek. You might hide under the bed. What if you read in the chair? You would be next to the desk.

Identify Circle the words in the text that describe different positions.

Quest Connection

Think of an obstacle that a person would have to climb. Describe the position of the person in relation to the ground.

Push or Pull

People use pushes and pulls in an obstacle course. People must push to complete some obstacles. They must pull to complete other obstacles.

Identify Which photo shows a pull? Which photo shows a push? Write the correct term under each photo.

_____

_____

Predict Imagine that the person drops the ball. What kind of force would the person use to pick it up?

_____

_____

How Objects Move

SC.2.P.13.4 Demonstrate that the greater the force (push or pull) applied to an object, the greater the change in motion of the object. (Also SC.2.N.1.2, LAFS.2.RI.3.8, LAFS. K12.R.1.1, MAFS.K12.MP.2.1, and MAFS.2.MD.2.5)

Vocabulary

speed

I can demonstrate that the way an object moves depends on the amount of force that is used.

Jumpstart Discovery!

Look at the ball in the photo. Predict what will happen when the ball makes contact with another object.

How can you change how fast or slow an object moves?

Scientists test how fast or slow an object can move. How can you make a ball change how fast or slow it moves?

Materials
- ball
- ramp
- stopwatch
- tape

Procedure

☐ **1.** Use all of the materials. Plan a way to **measure** how fast or slow the ball moves using forces. Show your plan to your teacher.

☐ **2.** Conduct your investigation. Do three trials. Record your data.

Science Practice

You **measure** to collect data and gather information.

Observations

Analyze and Interpret Data

3. Compare Compare your data with another group. Tell what happened when you used different amounts of force.

Change Direction

An object will change its motion in the direction it is pushed or pulled. Suppose you change the direction of the force. The object will move in a different direction.

Someone kicks a ball to you. The ball changes direction when you kick it back.

Recognize The girl pushes the scooter with her foot. She moves forward in a straight line. Write one way she could change the direction of the scooter.

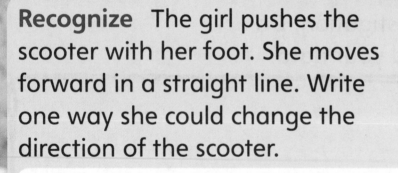

Fast and Slow

👆 **INTERACTIVITY**

Complete an activity on how objects move.

Speed is how fast or slow an object moves. An object will move faster if you apply more force. You apply more force when you push or pull harder. The object will move slower if you apply less force.

Identify Circle the correct force. The boy will move faster on the skateboard if he pushes softer/harder.

Quest Connection

Suppose that you have to climb a wall on an obstacle. You will pull yourself up a rope. Tell how you can pull yourself up the rope faster.

Far and Near

How far an object moves depends on how much force is used. It takes more force to move objects farther.

Suppose you wanted to make a baseball go far. Throw it hard. You have used more force. Watch how far it goes!

Suppose you wanted to make a baseball go a short distance. Toss it gently. You have used less force. It will not move far.

Illustrate Draw a picture of where a soccer ball stops when you kick it lightly. Draw where the ball stops when you kick it harder.

Math ▸ Toolbox

Compare Numbers
You kick a ball. It moves two meters. You kick the ball harder. It moves five meters. How much farther did the ball move the second time you kicked it? Which kick used more force?

MAFS.K12.MP.2.1, MAFS.2.MD.2.5

Player throws a baseball.

Amount of Force

People use different amounts of force to complete an obstacle course. Some obstacles require a harder push or pull. Look at the pictures.

Compare Which object do you think would require a stronger pull and push? Why?

_____

_____

_____

_____

Magnets

SC.2.P.13.2 Demonstrate that magnets can be used to make some things move without touching them. (Also **SC.2.P.8.1**, **SC.2.N.1.1**, **SC.2.N.1.2**, and **LAFS.2.RI.1.3**)

Vocabulary

magnet

attract

repel

I can demonstrate that magnets can push or pull some metal objects without touching them.

Jumpstart Discovery!

Talk about where there are magnets in your home. Make a list of uses for magnets.

uInvestigate Lab

How strong is a magnet?

Scientists use magnets to move objects without touching them. How can you test the strength of a magnet?

Procedure

☐ 1. Make a plan to test the strength of a magnet. Show your plan to your teacher.

☐ 2. Conduct your investigation. Record your data.

Trial	Observations and Measurements

Materials

• magnet

Suggested Materials

• paper clips
• metal washers
• metal marbles
• metric ruler

Science Practice

You **communicate** information to others to share your results.

Analyze and Interpret Data

3. **Communicate** your results and compare with another group's results. What do you notice?

_____

_____

_____

Magnets

A **magnet** can push or pull some metal objects. Magnets can **repel**, or push away from, other magnets. Magnets **attract**, or pull toward, some metal objects without touching them. Magnets attract metals like iron, nickel, and cobalt. Magnets do not attract plastic, paper, and wood.

A strong magnet can attract objects that are farther away. A weaker magnet must be closer to objects to attract them.

Differentiate The magnet attracts some objects. Circle these objects. The magnet does not attract some objects. Draw an X on these objects.

Science Practice
▶ Toolbox 🔧

Ask Questions Ask questions about attraction to magnets.

🔵 SC.2.N.1.1

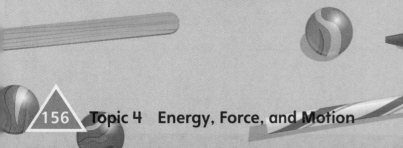

Magnet Poles

Magnets have poles. A pole has the strongest push or pull. Look at the poles of the magnets. The N is for north pole. The S is for south pole. Like poles repel. Opposite poles attract.

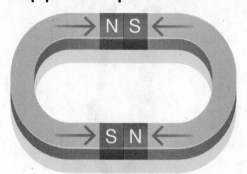

Quest Connection

People must swing on a rope for an obstacle. People must be able to reach the rope. Tell how you could design the obstacle. Tell how you could use a magnet to make the rope stay in place.

Uses of a Magnet

Magnets have force. People use forces in obstacle courses. Suppose that a large magnet is hanging above an obstacle. A person runs under the magnet. What would happen to the person?

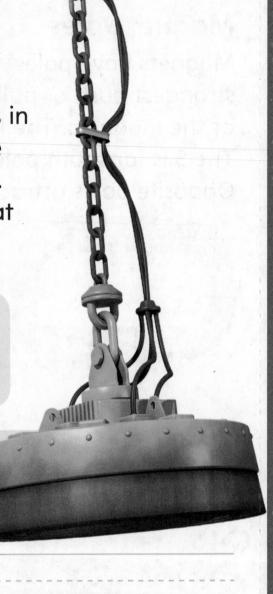

Analyze Tell what would happen if the person had car keys in his or her pocket and why.

Draw Conclusions Do you think magnets could be used in an obstacle course? Why or why not?

_____

_____

_____

_____

_____

_____

_____

_____

_____

How can we make a better magnet?

A magnetic field is the area all around a magnet. This area attracts some metal objects. Scientists use magnets for different research projects. They also use magnets to make sensors.

A 3D printer makes objects. The printer piles up layers of materials. Scientists can make magnets with 3D printers. They can make magnetic fields that have different shapes. These magnets are strong. They are stronger than magnets made in other ways. It costs less money to make them.

magnetic field

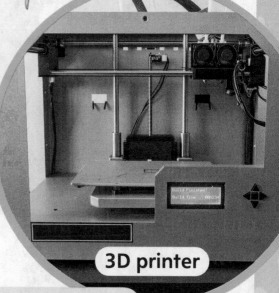

3D printer

☑ **Reading Check** Use Evidence from Text It is better to use a 3D printer to make a magnet. Underline evidence in the text that supports this idea.

Lesson 5

Gravity

SC.2.P.13.3 Recognize that objects are pulled toward the ground unless something holds them up. (Also **SC.2.N.1.1, SC.2.N.1.5, LAFS.2.RI.3.8,** and **LAFS.K12.R.1.1**)

Vocabulary

gravity

I can demonstrate that gravity pulls things toward the center of Earth.

Jumpstart Discovery!

Drop an eraser. Watch what happens. Tell your ideas about why things fall to the floor when dropped.

HANDS-ON LAB

SC.2.P.13.3, SC.2.N.1.5

How does the speed of two falling objects compare?

What happens if you drop a light object and a heavy object at the same time?

Material
• pan balance

Suggested Materials
• book
• penny
• domino

Procedure

☐ **1.** Make a plan to compare two falling objects.

☐ **2.** Predict what happens when you drop them.

_____

- - - - - - - - - - - - - - - - - - -

_____

☐ **3.** Show your plan to your teacher before you begin. **Collect data**. Record and circle it.

Science Practice

You **collect data** so you can draw accurate conclusions from your investigation.

Observations

Object	Weight	Speed
		faster, slower, same
		faster, slower, same

Analyze and Interpret Data

4. Draw Conclusions Tell how your prediction compared to your results.

Gravity

Gravity is a force that pulls things toward the center of Earth. Look at the dogs jumping into the air. They will not float up. Gravity will pull them down.

Think about when it rains. Gravity is the force that pulls the rain down to the ground.

Analyze Tell what would happen to the dogs if gravity did not exist.

Resisting Gravity

INTERACTIVITY

Complete an activity to investigate gravity.

You throw a ball up in the air. Then it starts to fall. Gravity pulls the ball down to Earth. Why did the ball go up?

The ball goes up because you push the ball. That force works against gravity. You do not keep pushing the ball. So the pull of gravity brings the ball back to Earth.

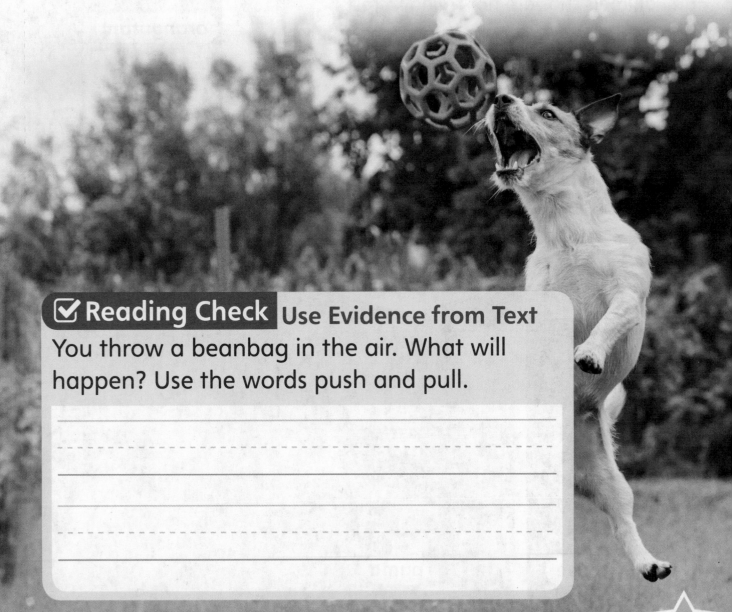

☑ **Reading Check** **Use Evidence from Text**

You throw a beanbag in the air. What will happen? Use the words push and pull.

_____

_____

_____

_____

_____

Pull of Gravity

Gravity pulls things toward the center of Earth unless something holds them up. Gravity pulls harder on objects that weigh more.

Visual Literacy

Circle any animals that are trying to resist gravity. Draw an X on any animals that are not trying to resist gravity. Tell why the orangutan does not fall to the ground.

orangutan

wood mouse

puma

African elephant and her calf

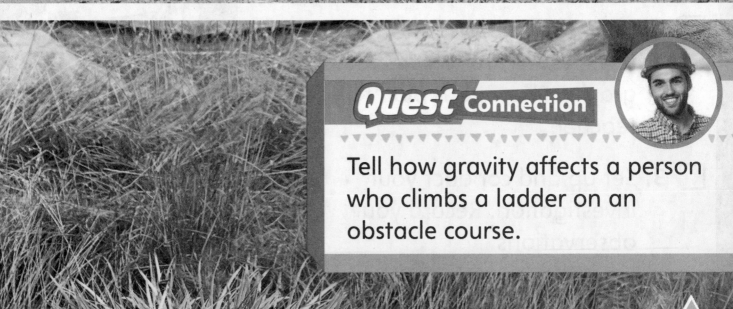

Quest Connection

Tell how gravity affects a person who climbs a ladder on an obstacle course.

How does **gravity** affect the way w a t e r flows?

Engineers observe how gravity affects things in nature. They can use their observations to help build structures like obstacle courses. How can you show how gravity affects water?

Materials
- container
- plastic cup
- water
- ramp

Suggested Materials
- soil
- sand

Procedure

☐ **1.** Think of ways you can use the materials to see how gravity affects water.

☐ **2. Plan your investigation** that tests how water is affected by gravity. Show your plan to your teacher.

☐ **3.** Set up and conduct your investigation. Record your observations.

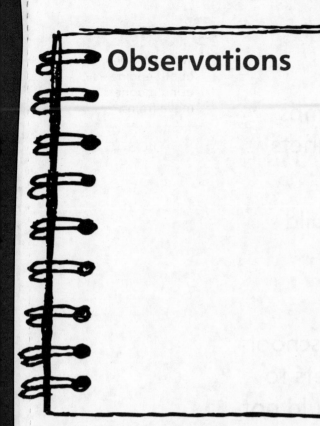

Observations

Analyze and Interpret Data

4. **Observe** Look at your data. How did gravity affect water?

5. **Design** How can water be used in an obstacle course?

SC.2.P.13.1, SC.2.P.13.2, SC.2.P.13.3, SC.2.P.13.4, SC.2.N.1.6

▶ **VIDEO**

Watch a video about engineers using magnets to move trains.

Design a Toy Car!

Some toy cars are built to go up ramps with the help of magnets. The magnets help the toy cars fight gravity.

Would you like to help engineers build toy cars?

Build It

Build a model of a toy car for your school playground. The car will use magnets to move up a ramp. The magnets should not touch the car to move it.

☐ Think of how to use magnets to move the model car up the ramp.

☐ Draw a design of the model car. Draw a design of the ramp it will go up. Make a plan to test your model car. Show your design and your plan to your teacher.

☐ Gather materials. Build the model car. Build the ramp.

☐ Test the model car. Think of ways you could improve your model. Write them in the box.

Design the Toy Car

Ways to Improve Your Model

INTERACTIVITY

Apply what you learned in the Quest.

STEM # Design an Obstacle Course

What forces are at work in an obstacle course?

Think about energy, force, and motion. Think of how each will help you design the obstacle course.

Show What You Found

It is time for you to plan an obstacle course. The course is for a school playground. Use what you have learned about types of energy. Use what you have learned about force and how objects move. Use what you have learned about magnets and gravity. Design the obstacles you will include in your course. Make a drawing of the course.

QUEST CHECK ✓ OFF

Civil Engineer

Civil engineers plan, design, and build structures. Some are large structures. They may build airports, bridges, roads, dams, and canals. Some are smaller structures. They may build obstacle courses.

Civil engineers decide what materials to use when building. They think about the costs of the materials. They use computers to draw designs.

What would you like to design and build if you were a civil engineer? Explain why.

_____

_____

_____

_____

The Essential Question

What are some ways different objects can move?

Show What You Learned

Tell a partner two ways that an object can move. How can you change the way an object moves?

Read each question and choose or write the best answer.

1. For each action, write whether each force needs a "weak" or "strong" force.

Action	Weak or strong force?
push a large truck	
make a marble roll slowly	
throw a ball very high	

2. Compare the difference in force that you need to make an object move a short distance and a long distance.

_____

_____

_____

_____

3. Jesse dropped his key into a hole. Why did he use a magnet, and not a hook, to reach the key?

    a. Magnets attract metal objects without touching them.

    b. Magnets push on objects and hooks pull on them.

    c. The hook would not be able to reach the key.

    d. The hook would repel and not attract the metal key.

4. Explain why the cat is being pulled toward the ground.

_____

_____

_____

_____

5. Describe one way people use electricity in their homes.

_____

_____

_____

Read the scenario and answer questions 1–2.

Four students pushed a ball up a ramp. The table shows the time it took each student to go up the ramp with the ball.

Student	Time to go up the ramp (seconds)
Alex	4
Jess	8
Rami	7
Eman	5

1 Which statement **best** explains the times shown in the table?

Ⓐ The texture of the ramp changed.

Ⓑ The ramp changed after each time it was used.

Ⓒ The students used different amounts of force.

Ⓓ Some of the students are tall and some are short.

2 If each student used more force in the next turn, what would change about how the ball moved on the ramp?

Ⓕ It would have more kinetic energy.

Ⓖ It would have more potential energy.

Ⓗ It would attract more energy.

Ⓘ It would change direction.

Read the scenario and answer questions 3–4.

Jon drew a diagram of a roller coaster.

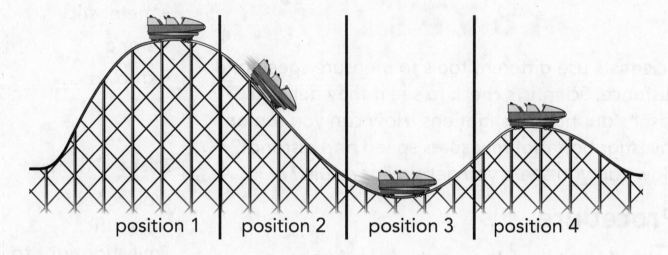

position 1   position 2   position 3   position 4

3 What force causes the roller coaster car to move downhill on the track?
  Ⓐ magnets
  Ⓑ gravity
  Ⓒ electricity
  Ⓓ fuel

4 Which position is the car moving the fastest?
  Ⓕ position 1
  Ⓖ position 2
  Ⓗ position 3
  Ⓘ position 4

uDemonstrate Lab

How does speed affect how far an object m o v e s ?

Scientists use different tools to measure speed and distance. Scientists check to see if they get similar results during investigations. How can you run an investigation that measures speed and distance? How can you see if you get similar results?

Materials
- toy car
- meter stick
- string
- stopwatch

Science Practice

You **repeat scientific investigations** to see how results compare.

Procedure

☐ **1.** Use all of the materials. Make a plan to measure how far and how fast the toy car travels. Make sure your plan includes a way to check for similar results.

☐ **2.** Show your plan to your teacher.

☐ **3.** Conduct your investigation. Record your data. **Repeat your investigation.**

Observations

Analyze and Interpret Data

4. **Interpret Data** Were your results similar or different in each trial? Explain.

_____

_____

_____

5. **Evaluate** What would happen if you changed the amount of force used?

_____

_____

_____

Topic 5

Plants and Animals

SC.2.L.14.1 Distinguish human body parts (brain, heart, lungs, stomach, muscles, and skeleton) and their basic functions. **SC.2.L.16.1** Observe and describe major stages in life cycles of plants and animals, including beans and butterflies. **SC.2.L.17.1** Compare and contrast the basic needs that all living things, including humans, have for survival. (Also **SC.2.N.1.1, SC.2.N.1.2, SC.2.N.1.3, SC.1.N.1.5, LAFS.2.RI.1.1, LAFS.2.RI.1.2, LAFS.2.RI.1.3** and **MAFS.2.OA.2**)

Go online to access
your digital course.

▶ VIDEO

📖 eTEXT

👆 INTERACTIVITY

▶ SCIENCE SONG

🎮 GAME

☑ ASSESSMENT

The Essential Question

What do animals and plants need to survive?

Show What You Know

Does this animal get its food from plants or other animals? Tell how you know.

Quest Kickoff

Help Make a Healthcare Guide

How can we best meet the needs of the plants and animals in our care?

Hi! My name is Mr. Larsen. I am a biologist. I need help taking care of all the animals and plants at the wildlife sanctuary. It takes many people to care for all the living things at the wildlife sanctuary. In this activity, you will make a healthcare plan. You can choose any plant or animal you want! You can even choose yourself!

The path shows the Quest activities you will complete as you work through the topic. Check off your progress each time you complete an activity with a 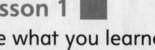 QUEST CHECK ✓ OFF .

Quest Check-In 1

Lesson 1

Use what you learned about life cycles. Think about what a living thing needs during different life stages.

SC.2.L.17.1 Compare and contrast the basic needs that all living things, including humans, have for survival.

VIDEO
Watch a video about a biologist.

Quest Findings

Complete the Quest! Think of a creative way that you can design a healthcare guide.

Quest Check-In 4

Lesson 4 ▲

Use what you learned about humans to explore what our body parts need to live.

Quest Check-In 3

Lesson 3 ◆

Identify plants that animals eat.

Quest Check-In Lab 2

Lesson 2 ●

Find out how plants meet their needs.

What do living things need?

Scientists make observations that can be used to describe objects. How do you know if something is living or nonliving?

Procedure

☐ 1. **Observe** the objects.

☐ 2. Describe the objects. Tell if each needs food, air, water, or space to live.

☐ 3. Sort the objects as living or nonliving.

Analyze and Interpret Data

4. **Compare** your observations with another group. How are your groups of objects alike? How are they different?

_____

_____

_____

_____

Suggested Materials

- rock
- windup toy
- plant
- fish in water
- stuffed animal
- artificial flower

Science Practice

You **observe** to describe things.

Compare and Contrast

 GAME

Practice what you learn with the Mini Games.

Biologists study all living things. Plants and animals are living things.

To compare means to look for things that are similar. To contrast means to look for things that are different.

Living Things

Living things can grow and use food for energy. Plants and animals can both grow. Plants and animals both need food. Plants make their own food, and animals must find food to eat. Some animals eat plants. Some animals eat other animals.

☑ **Reading Check** **Compare and Contrast** Find another reading about living things. Are the important points the same in the two readings?

_____

_____

_____

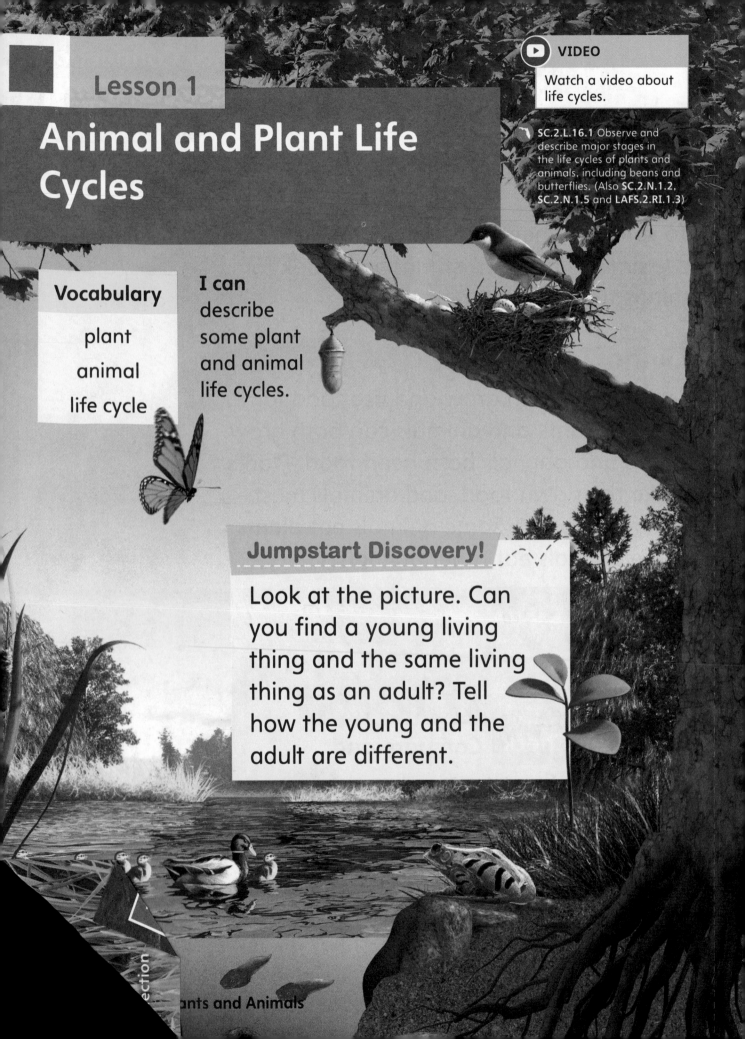

▶ **VIDEO**

Watch a video about life cycles.

SC.2.L.16.1 Observe and describe major stages in the life cycles of plants and animals, including beans and butterflies. (Also **SC.2.N.1.2, SC.2.N.1.5** and **LAFS.2.RI.1.3**)

Vocabulary

plant

animal

life cycle

I can describe some plant and animal life cycles.

Jumpstart Discovery!

Look at the picture. Can you find a young living thing and the same living thing as an adult? Tell how the young and the adult are different.

ants and Animals

What is inside a seed or a bulb?

Some plants grow from seeds. A bean is a seed. Other plants grow from bulbs. Explore the inside of beans and bulbs.

Materials

- tulip bulb (cut in half)
- lima bean (cut in half)
- hand lens

Procedure

☐ **1.** Look at the cut bulb and the cut bean.

☐ **2.** Find the tiny young plant. Draw what you see.

Science Practice

You **infer** when you draw a conclusion from observations.

⚠ Wash your hands.

Analyze and Interpret Data

3. Infer What do you think the other parts of the seed and bulb do for the young plant?

_____

_____

_____

Plants and Animals

A **plant** is a living thing that can use energy from the sun to make food for itself. A plant grows in one place. It absorbs water and nutrients from the soil.

An **animal** is a living thing that cannot make its own food. An animal must eat. Dogs, birds, insects, and goats are all animals. Some animals eat plants. Some eat animals. Some eat both plants and animals.

☑ **Reading Check**

Compare and Contrast Underline how plants and animals are similar. Circle how they are different.

goat

Quest Connection

Tell how caring for a plant or animal may change throughout its life cycle.

Cycles

ants and Animals

Plant Life Cycles

The way plants and other living things grow and change is called a **life cycle**. The life cycles of many plants start with a seed. A seed contains what will become a small young plant.

A seed contains food to help the seedling start growing. A root grows from the seedling. The root grows down into the ground. It gets water for the seedling. The young plant grows leaves. It starts to grow toward the sun. It gets energy from the sun. The adult plant grows flowers that turn into fruit. Seeds are inside the fruit. These seeds start the cycle again.

adult plant

seeds

seedling

young plant

Butterfly Life Cycle

The caterpillar eats many leaves and grows.

Visual Literacy

Draw arrows to show the direction of the monarch butterfly life cycle.

The caterpillar hatches from an egg.

INTERACTIVITY

Go online to learn more about the life cycles of plants and animals.

The caterpillar stops eating and forms a chrysalis.

After ten to fourteen days, it becomes an adult butterfly. It drinks nectar from flowers for food.

Animal Life Cycles

Animals have life cycles. An animal is born, grows into an adult, has young, and dies.

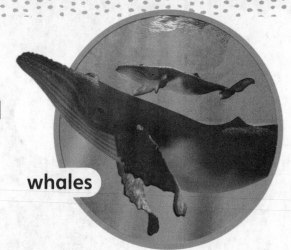
whales

Animal life cycles begin with an egg. For some animals, the egg is inside the mother. The mother will give birth to the baby. A whale gives birth to her calf.

For other animals, the egg is outside of the mother. The young will hatch from the egg. A turtle is hatched from an egg.

turtles

Some animals, like turtles, are born looking like their parents. Other animals, like frogs, look different at birth.

tadpole

Literacy ▸ Toolbox

Compare and Contrast Circle words that describe where a whale's egg _____ Underline where a turtle's _____.

Cycles

nts and Animals

frog

Care Throughout the Life Cycle

Young plants and animals have different needs than adults do.

Observe the living things. Match the young plant or animal with the adult.

Describe Choose the plant or the animal. What care does it need at the start of the life cycle?

_____

_____

QUEST CHECK

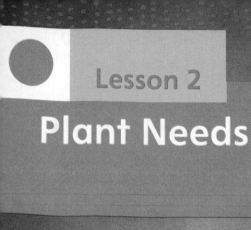

Lesson 2

Plant Needs

▶ **VIDEO**

Watch a video about how a plant grows.

SC.2.L.17.1 Compare and contrast the basic needs that all living things, including humans, have for survival. (Also **SC.2.N.1.1, SC.2.N.1.2,** and **SC.2.N.1.3**)

Vocabulary

nutrient

I can explain that plants need sunlight, air, water, space, and nutrients.

Jumpstart Discovery!

Do you or does someone you know take care of plants? Tell a partner something do to take care of plants.

HANDS-ON LAB

SC.2.L.17.1, SC.2.N.1.1

What do plants need to grow?

Biologists make sure plants are healthy and have the things they need to grow. What do you think plants need?

Materials
- plants
- water

Science Practice

You plan an investigation to answer a question.

Procedure

☐ 1. **Plan an investigation** to test whether plants need sunlight or water to grow.

☐ 2. Show your design to your teacher.

☐ 3. Set up and begin your investigation. Check your plants each day.

Analyze and Interpret Data

4. **Compare** your plants with the plants of other groups. Tell what you notice.

5. **Compare** how the needs of plants compare with the needs of other living things.

What Plants Need

A plant needs energy from sunlight. It uses sunlight, air, water and nutrients from the soil to make food and oxygen. A **nutrient** is a material that helps living things grow. Nutrients and sunlight help the plant make food.

The plant uses the food it makes to grow. Plants that do not get what they need will not grow well. Plants without enough space will be small. If a plant does not get what it needs for a long time, it may die.

Identify Put an **X** on
lants need to live.

Needs

nts and Animals

Plant Parts

Plants have parts that help them get what they need to make food and grow. All plants have roots, stems, and leaves.

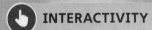

INTERACTIVITY

Go online to learn more about how plant parts help plants meet their needs.

Roots help the plant stay in the soil. They also help the plant get the water and nutrients it needs to grow. Stems carry water and nutrients from the roots to the leaves. They also carry the food the leaves make to other parts of the plant. Stems also help the plant to stand up. Leaves catch sunlight and air to make food for the plant. Leaves also make oxygen that animals and people need.

☑ **Reading Check** **Compare and Contrast** Circle three things that all plants have.

Quest Connection

▼▼▼▼▼▼▼▼▼▼▼▼▼▼▼▼▼▼▼▼▼▼▼▼

What should a guide about plants say about something plants nee

How can you see the parts of a plant **work?**

Most plants have roots, stems, and leaves. How do they work?

Materials

- potted plant
- carrot with leaves
- celery with leaves
- food coloring
- water
- cup

Procedure

☐ 1. **Observe** the carrot and the potted plant. Identify any roots, stems, or leaves.

☐ 2. Make a plan to observe how water and nutrients move from one part of the plant to another. Use the materials you have not yet used. Show your teacher.

☐ 3. Conduct your investigation.

☐ 4. Compare your observations with another group.

Science Practice

You **observe** to learn more about things.

⚠ Do not taste any thing in the lab.

...Needs

...nts and Animals

Analyze and Interpret Data

5. **Compare** How was the potted plant like the carrot?

_____

_____

_____

_____

_____

6. **Explain** How do you know water moves through plants?

_____

_____

_____

_____

7. **Evaluate** Why is it important to know about plant parts for a healthcare guide?

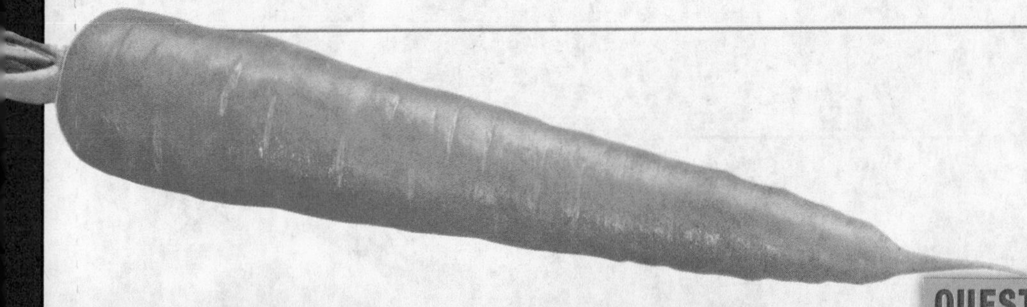

_____

_____

_____

_____

_____

Animal Needs

▶ **VIDEO**

Watch a video about animal needs.

SC.2.L.17.1 Compare and contrast the basic needs that all living things, including humans, have for survival. (Also, SC.2.N.1.1, and, MAFS.2.OA.2.2)

Vocabulary

shelter

I can explain that animals need food, oxygen, water, and shelter.

Jumpstart Discovery!

Do you have a pet? How do you care for that pet? Act like a pet you have or that you want. See if a classmate can guess what that pet needs.

What do **animals** need?

All animals have needs. How can you meet the needs of a small pet?

Science Practice

You **ask questions** to find out what living things need to live.

Procedure

☐ 1. Think of a pet you have or would like to have.

☐ 2. Consider what the animal needs for shelter, food, air, and water.

☐ 3. Make a list of things you need to take care of it.

Analyze and Interpret Data

4. **Explain** What will your animal eat?

_____
_____
_____

5. **Describe** What kind of shelter does your animal need?

_____
_____
_____

6. **Evaluate** What else will your animal need?

_____
_____
_____

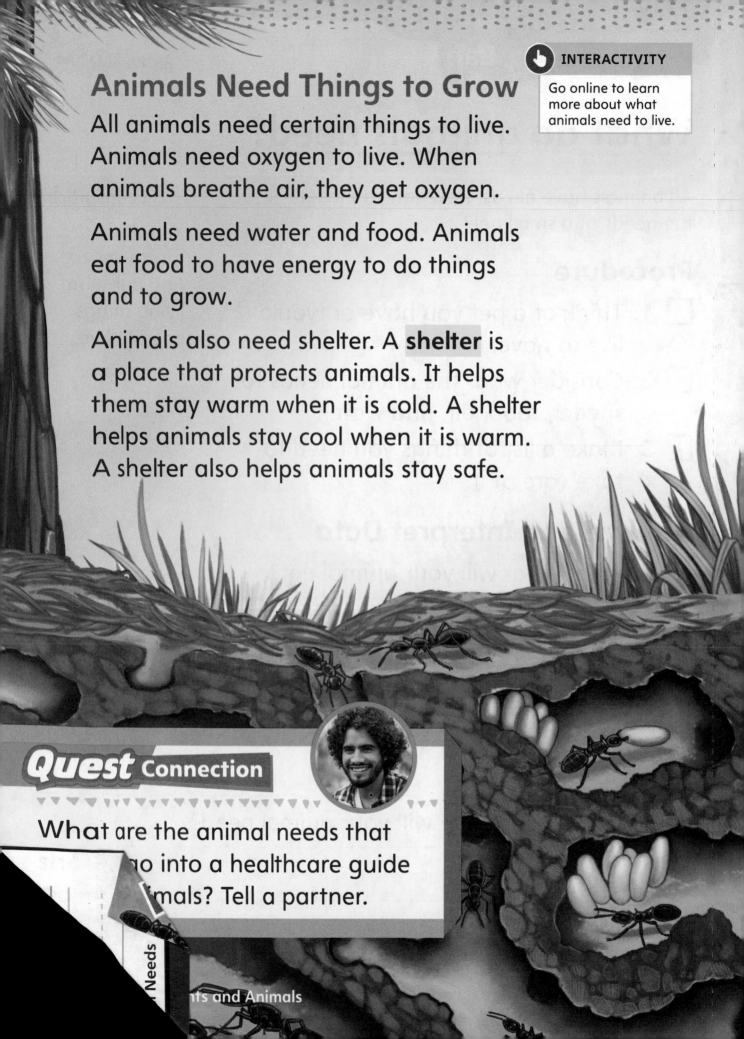

Animals Need Things to Grow

INTERACTIVITY

Go online to learn more about what animals need to live.

All animals need certain things to live. Animals need oxygen to live. When animals breathe air, they get oxygen.

Animals need water and food. Animals eat food to have energy to do things and to grow.

Animals also need shelter. A **shelter** is a place that protects animals. It helps them stay warm when it is cold. A shelter helps animals stay cool when it is warm. A shelter also helps animals stay safe.

Quest Connection

What are the animal needs that ___ go into a healthcare guide ___mals? Tell a partner.

Needs

ts and Animals

Animals Need Space to Move

Animals must also be able to move. Animals may run, hop, walk, fly, swim, or swing from trees.

Animals need space to move. Some animals need a large space. A wolf needs a large space to hunt. Some animals only need a small space. An ant does not need much space.

Math ▸ Toolbox

Subtract A big fish needs a 20 gallon tank. A small snail needs a 10 gallon tank. How much bigger does the tank for the fish need to be?

MAFS.2.OA.2.2

☑ **Reading Check** **Compare and Contrast** How are a wolf and an ant alike? How are they different?

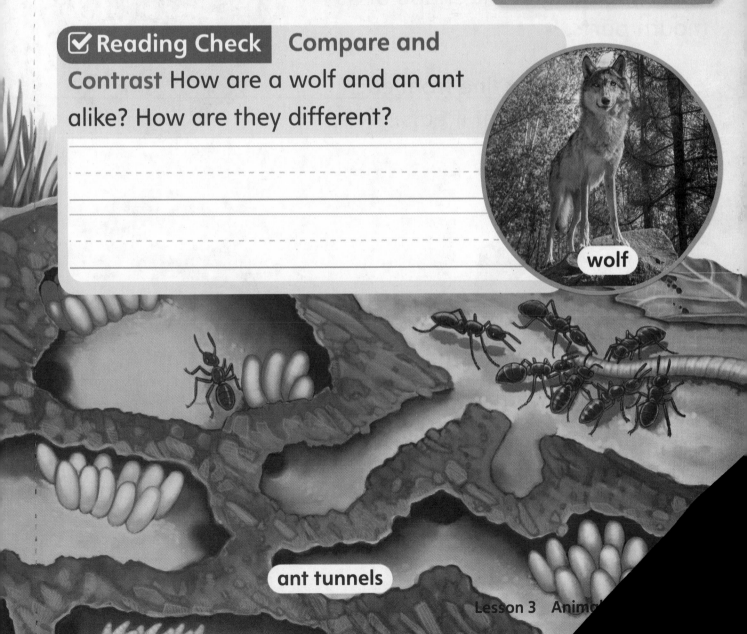

wolf

ant tunnels

Some Animals Need Plants

Some animals use plants for food. Some animals eat plants. Some animals drink a sugary liquid called nectar from a plant's flowers. You can sometimes tell what an animal eats by looking at the shape of its mouth parts.

Identify Draw a line from each animal to the plant it eats.

Compare What is similar about ese animals eat?

_____

_____

Needs

EXTREME SCIENCE

Snow Leopards

Snow leopards live high in the mountains in Central Asia. They live on very high, rocky mountains.

Snow leopards eat other animals. They use their sense of smell to find food. They also leave their own scent. Their own scent is a message to other snow leopards.

In the zoo, zookeepers keep snow leopards healthy. Zookeepers give them high, rocky places to live. They hide food in high places. Snow leopards need to climb to find the food.

Biologists mark trails with smells to help the snow leopards find their food.

Describe How do snow leopards use their senses to find food?

_____

_____

_____

Lesson 4

Human Body

Vocabulary

brain
heart
lungs
stomach
muscles
skeleton

I can describe what the brain, heart, lungs, stomach, muscles and skeleton do.

Jumpstart Discovery!

You use many parts when you run. Make a list of all the body parts you can think of. Can you name some of the parts inside your body that you use when you run?

How can you make a model of your (body?)

Biologists use models of the human body to help them observe the body. How can you make a model of the body?

Materials
- butcher paper
- crayons

Procedure

☐ 1. Look at the materials.

☐ 2. Make a plan to use the materials to make a model of a human body. Show your teacher.

☐ 3. Make your model.

☐ 4. Do you know any parts that are inside the body? Draw them.

Science Practice

You can **use models** to understand how things work.

Analyze and Interpret Data

5. **Compare** How is your drawing like a real-life body?

_____

_____

6. **Evaluate** What is something a real human body does that your model does not do?

_____

_____

One Body, Many Parts

Human bodies can do amazing things. A system is group of parts that work together. Your body is made of parts that work together. You will learn about the body on these pages.

The **skeleton** holds the body together, helps it move, and protects it. It is made of 206 bones. Bones cannot move by themselves. **Muscles** are body parts that help us move. They make the bones move. There are more than 600 muscles in your body. Your **heart** is a muscle that pumps blood through the body.

☑ **Reading Check** **Compare and Contrast** Both muscles and bones help you move. Tell how are they different.

INTERACTIVITY

Go online to learn more about how human body parts work together.

Quest Connection

What do you need to live that plants and animals also need to live?

 206 Topic 5 **Plants and Animals**

Math ▸ Toolbox 🔧

Measure Length
Measure the length of your arm from your wrist to your elbow to the nearest centimeter. Measure from your elbow from your shoulder. Which part is longer?

🇺🇸 MAFS.2.MD.1.1

Blood carries oxygen through your body. **Lungs** are organs that help us breathe air. They get bigger as you breathe in air through your mouth or nose. Oxygen from the air passes through our lungs to our blood. Blood also carries nutrients from the food you eat through your body.

Your **stomach** is a body part that helps break down food into nutrients. Your **brain** is the organ that controls everything your body does. It causes your body to move and your heart to pump. It also allows you to breathe without thinking.

Explain Tell how the heart and lungs work together.

Use It and Move It

Many body parts are used in every activity you do. What is going on in your body when you move?

This biologist has to walk many miles around the wildlife sanctuary. She checks to make sure the animals and plants have what they need.

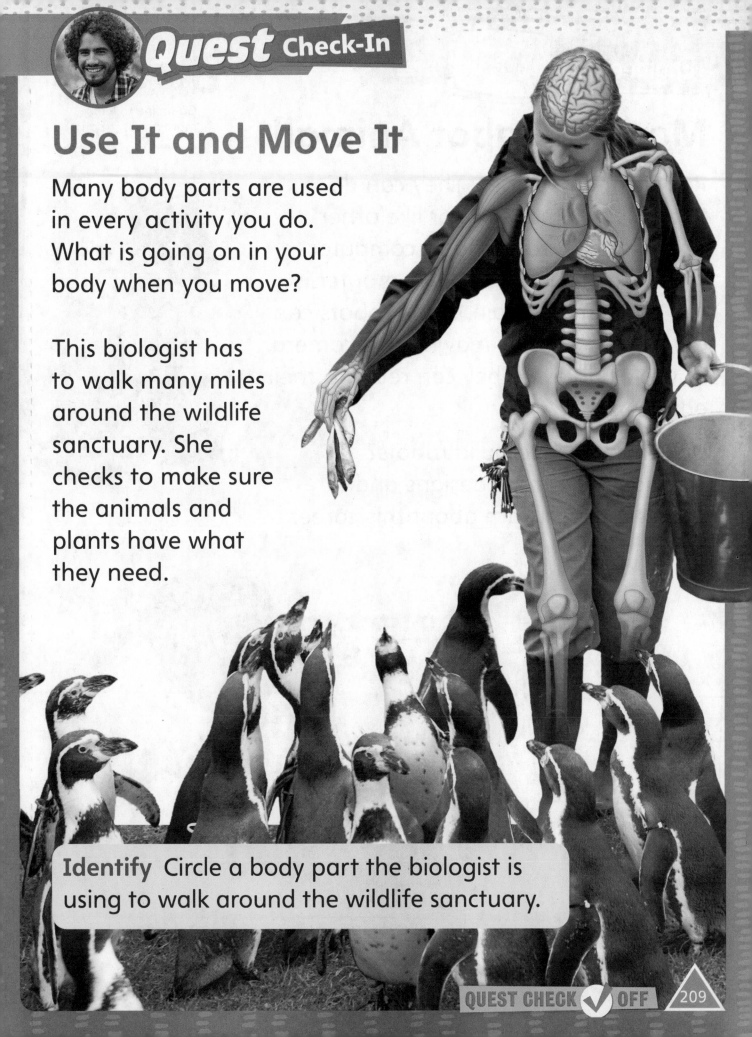

Identify Circle a body part the biologist is using to walk around the wildlife sanctuary.

INTERACTIVITY

Go online to learn more about robotics.

Model a Robot Animal!

Robots are machines. They can do things like humans do, or like other animals do. A robot has a computer to control its actions. The computer is like an animal's brain. Some robots can detect things. They may have a camera to use as an eye. They can react to their environments.

Would you like to build robots? A robotics engineer designs and makes robots. Learn about this career.

Model It

Compare how the brain of an animal is like the computer of a robot.

☐ Decide what you would like your robot to do. What parts does the robot need?

_____

- - - - - - - - - - - - - - - - -

_____

- - - - - - - - - - - - - - - - -

_____

☐ Draw your robot. Identify and label the part that is like an animal's brain. Label the parts that are like other parts of an animal.

☐ Tell how the robot's "brain" controls the other parts.

Help Make a Healthcare Guide

How can we best meet the needs of the plants and animals in our care?

Now you can choose what plant or animal you would like to care for! What are some of the things the plant or animal you chose needs to survive? How do those needs compare to yours?

_____

_____

_____

Show What You Found

Make the healthcare guide for your living thing. Be creative! Use the things that your plant or animal needs to help plan your guide.

QUEST CHECK ✓ OFF

Biologist

Biologists study living things. Biologists usually pick one group of living things to study. They may help farmers learn about growing crops. They may develop new plants that have many flowers.

Some biologists travel to faraway places. They might discover unknown plants and animals. Biologists might even study how plants and animals interact. Biologists are important because we depend on plants and animals for things we need like oxygen and food.

If you were a biologist, what question would you like to study?

_____

- -

_____

_____

- -

_____

The Essential Question

What do animals and plants need to survive?

Show What You Learned
Tell a partner what you learned about plant and animal needs.

Read each question and choose or write the best answer.

1. Describe two ways that a plant could help a lizard survive in its environment.

_____

- -

_____

- -

_____

2. How do parts of a plant help it get what it needs? Use the word bank to fill in the table.

| leaves | stems | roots |

Plant part	What it does
	collect sunlight
	take in water and nutrients from soil
	bring water and nutrients to leaves

3. Draw in the stages of the plant life cycle.

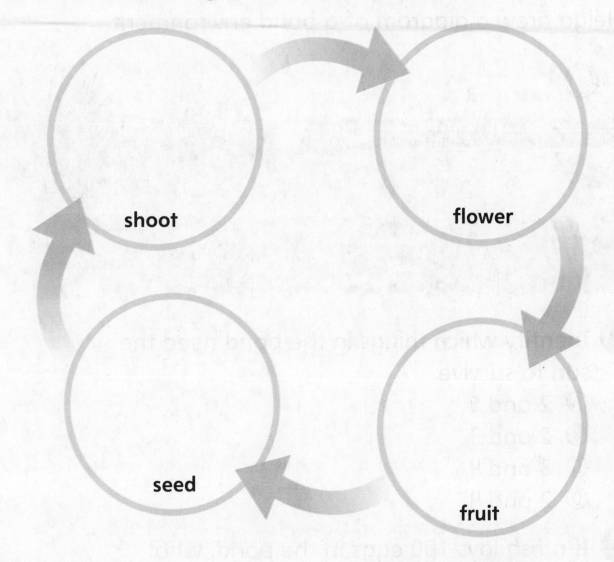

shoot

flower

seed

fruit

4. Which part of your body works closely with your lungs to help your whole body get oxygen?
   a. muscles
   b. skeleton
   c. heart
   d. stomach

Read the scenario and answer questions 1–2.

Helga drew a diagram of a pond environment.

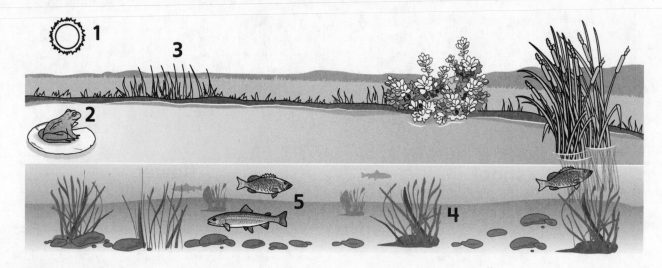

❶ Identify which things in the pond need the sun to survive.

   Ⓐ 2 and 5

   Ⓑ 2 and 3

   Ⓒ 3 and 4

   Ⓓ 2 and 4

❷ If a fish lays 100 eggs in the pond, what would the young fish need that the plants can provide?

   Ⓕ oxygen and space

   Ⓖ space and water

   Ⓗ oxygen and food

   Ⓘ food and water

Read the scenario and answer questions 3–4.

George drew two models of different life cycles.

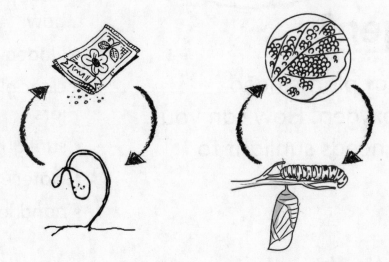

3 Describe how George should revise his models of the different life cycles.

   Ⓐ He should add a longer growth stage to each life cycle model.

   Ⓑ He should add the adult stage to each life cycle model.

   Ⓒ He should combine the life cycle models.

   Ⓓ He should remove the first stage of each life cycle model.

4 If a seedling needs sunlight but does not get any, what would happen to the plant?

   Ⓕ It would not be able to grow well.

   Ⓖ It would need extra water to grow.

   Ⓗ It would move to a new space.

   Ⓘ It would make more seeds.

How does a plant make oxygen?

Biologists know that plants need sunlight to make oxygen. How can you show that a plant needs sunlight to make oxygen?

Procedure

☐ **1.** Make a plan to show that plants need sunlight to make oxygen.

☐ **2.** Show your plan to your teacher.

☐ **3.** Conduct your investigation.

Materials

- clear plastic bowl
- Elodea
- clear plastic jars
- sunlight
- water
- hand lens

Observations

Analyze and Interpret Data

4. **Explain** How can you tell that oxygen is being released?

_____

_ _

_____

5. **Draw Conclusions** How do you know plants need sunlight?

_____

_ _

_____

Habitats

SC.2.L.17.2 Recognize and explain that living things are found all over Earth, but each is only able to live in habitats that meet its basic needs. (Also SC.2.N.1.1, SC.2.N.1.2, SC.2.N.1.3, SC.2.N.1.6, LAFS.2.RI.1.1, LAFS.2.RI.1.2, and MAFS.2.OA.1.1)

Go online to access
your digital course.

▶ VIDEO

📖 eTEXT

👆 INTERACTIVITY

▶ SCIENCE SONG

🎮 GAME

☑ ASSESSMENT

The Essential Question How do habitats support living things?

Show What You Know

Circle the needs of the living things in the picture.

Protect a Habitat

Why protect a local habitat?

Hi! My name is Mr. Rollins. I am an ecologist. I study plants and animals. I study the places they live. I work to protect these places.

I will be talking to city officials. Help me give them reasons to protect a local habitat. You will choose the habitat. You will explain why a habitat is important. Habitats meet the needs of living things. Use what you learn about habitats.

The path shows the Quest activities you will complete. Check off your progress each time you complete an activity with a QUEST CHECK ✓ OFF.

SC.2.L.17.2 Recognize and explain that living things are found all over Earth, but each is only able to live in habitats that meet its basic needs.

SC.2.N.1.1 Raise questions about the natural world, investigate them in teams through free exploration and systematic observations, and generate appropriate explanations based on those explorations.

SC.2.N.1.2 Compare the observations made by different groups using the same tools.

SC.2.N.1.6 Explain how scientists alone or in groups are always investigating new ways to solve problems.

Quest Check-In Lab 1

Lesson 1 ■
Model a plant with waxy leaves and a plant without waxy leaves. Decide which habitats would be best for the plants.

▶ VIDEO
Watch a video about an ecologist.

Quest Check-In 2

Lesson 2 ●
Explore the diversity of two land habitats.

Quest Check-In 3

Lesson 3 ◆
Investigate why some animals live in water habitats.

Quest Findings

Complete the Quest! Find a way to help Mr. Rollins protect a local habitat.

What is **out there?**

Scientists learn about different areas by observing them. How can you observe living and nonliving things in an area near you?

Suggested Materials

- hand lens
- collecting jar
- ruler

Procedure

☐ 1. As a class you will observe an area near you. How can you observe living and nonliving things in the area?

_____

_____

☐ 2. Choose materials to use. **Observe** the area. Collect data on living and nonliving things.

Science Practice

Scientists **make observations** to understand details about something.

Analyze and Interpret Data

3. **Explain** Tell how many different kinds of living things you observed.

4. **Infer** How do you think nonliving things help living things in the area?

_____

_____

_____

Main Idea and Details

Scientists study different areas. Read about the main idea and details of tide pools.

LAFS2.RI.1.1

 GAME

Practice what you learn with the Mini Games.

The main idea is what the sentences are about. Details tell about the main idea.

Tide Pools

Tide pools provide a home for many animals. A tide pool is an area found on some sea shores. The tides fill rocky areas with water. The water stays when the tide goes out. Small living things get trapped in the tide pools. They find the resources they need to survive.

✓ **Reading Check** **Main Idea and Details**
Tell where tide pools are found. Tell how they form. Use details from the text.

Tide pools with water at low tide

Identify Habitats

▶ VIDEO

Watch a video about habitats.

SC.2.L.17.2 Recognize and explain that living things are found all over Earth, but each is only able to live in habitats that meet its basic needs. (Also SC.2.N.1.1, LAFS2.RI.1.1, and LAFS.2.RI.1.2)

Vocabulary

habitat

diversity

adaptation

I can explain that plants and animals get what they need from their habitats.

I can identify different habitats.

Jumpstart Discovery!

Look at the habitat. Act out an animal that might live there. Ask a partner to guess. Take turns.

Who lives in a grassland?

Scientists study which plants and animals live in a place to learn more about the needs of living things. How do living things use the resources in that place?

Procedure

☐ 1. **Observe** the Grassland sheet.

☐ 2. What do living things need to live in the grassland?

_____

_____

_____

_____

☐ 3. Use the Who lives in a grassland? sheet. Cut out the living things whose needs are met by a grassland. Paste them on the grassland.

Analyze and Interpret Data

4. Tell what living things you included and did not include. Why?

Materials

- Grassland Sheet
- Who lives in a grassland? Sheet
- glue stick
- scissors

Science Practice

You **observe** when you look closely at things.

 Be careful when handling scissors.

Habitats

Living things are found all over Earth. They live in different habitats. A **habitat** is a place where a plant or animal lives. Habitats give living things their basic needs.

Habitats can be on land or in water. Some habitats are large. Others are small. The ocean, a forest, and a prairie are large habitats. The soil below a rock is a small habitat.

Compare and Contrast Draw an animal that would live in this water habitat. Tell how this animal would be like other animals in the picture. Tell how the animal would be different from the other animals.

Living Things and Their Habitats

Land and water habitats support living things in different ways. **Diversity** is how many different plants and animals live in a place.

Adaptations are characteristics of a living thing that help it survive in its habitat. For example, fish have gills. Gills help fish breathe underwater. A fish lives in a coral reef. The fish is colorful. Color is an adaptation. It helps the fish survive.

INTERACTIVITY

Complete an activity about living things and their habitats.

Literacy ► Toolbox 🔧

Main Idea and Details Read about living things and their habitats. Underline the main idea. Circle one detail.

LAFS2.RI.1.1, LAFS.2.RI.1.2

coral reef

Quest Connection

Describe a habitat near your school or home. Why should the habitat be protected?

Which <u>habitat</u> is (best?)

Scientists collect and compare data about a plant to learn about its habitat. What data can you collect to learn about the habitat of plants with waxy leaves and plants without waxy leaves?

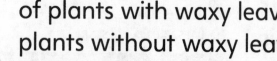

Materials
- waxed paper
- spray bottle with water
- Leaf Shapes
- scissors
- 2 paper towels

Science Practice

Scientist **compare data** with other scientists to check their results.

Procedure

☐ 1. Use all the materials. Make a plan to show how water affects a plant that has waxy leaves and a plant that does not have waxy leaves.

☐ 2. Show your plan to your teacher. Record your observations. **Compare your data** with another group.

⚠ **Be careful when handling scissors.**

Observations

Analyze and Interpret Data

3. **Compare** What did your data show about the habitats for plants with and without waxy leaves?

_____

_ _

_____

4. **Infer** Choose one of the plant types. How could you protect the habitat where it is found?

_____

_ _

_____

_____

_____

_ _

_____

uEngineer It! Define STEM

▶ VIDEO

Watch a video about planning a habitat to grow plants on Mars.

Plan a Habitat on Mars!

Some scientists want people to live on Mars. Remember that people need food and water. They need shelter and air. Habitats on Mars do not have those resources.

If people could grow food on Mars it would solve a big problem! But plants cannot grow on Mars. There are no nutrients or water in the soil. How can you help solve this problem?

Define It

Now plan a habitat for plants on Mars. Describe the things that plants need to survive.

☐ Brainstorm some features that a habitat on Mars would need to have.

It should	It should not

Draw a solution that would help plants survive on Mars. Label the parts of your solution.

Describe how your solution helps solve the problem.

Share your plan with a partner. Tell how your plan would help people live on Mars.

Living Things in Land Habitats

VIDEO

Watch a video about extreme land habitats.

SC.2.L.17.2 Recognize and explain that living things are found all over Earth, but each is only able to live in habitats that meet its basic needs. (Also SC.2.N.1.2, LAFS2.RI.1.1, and LAFS.2.RI.1.2)

Vocabulary

tundra

I can identify where plants and animals live on land.

Jumpstart Discovery!

Look at the picture. Circle five animals that live in this forest.

uInvestigate Lab

What do land plants need?

Scientists can model a habitat to study living things. How can you find out what type of habitat is best for a plant?

Materials

- radish seeds
- soil
- water
- plastic cups
- gloves

Procedure

☐ 1. Plan a way to compare how a plant will grow on land and in water. Show your plan to your teacher. Follow your plan.

☐ 2. Observe how the seeds grow for ten days. Record your observations.

Science Practice

Scientists **communicate** with other scientists to share their findings and ideas.

Day	Seeds in Soil	Seeds in Water

 Wash your hands after handling plant seeds and soil.

Analyze and Interpret Data

3. **Communicate** your results with another group. Tell what the plants need and which habitat is best.

Forests

Different types of forests grow all over the world. Tropical rain forests grow in warm, sunny areas. It rains often. They are the most diverse land habitat. Other forests have trees with leaves that turn colors in the fall. The leaves fall off the trees in the winter. The leaves grow back in spring. Temperatures change from season to season.

Deserts

Deserts are dry. They get very little rain. Few plants and animals grow in deserts. Desert plants like cacti have adaptations. For example, they have waxy coverings. These waxy coverings help them retain water.

Tundra

Arctic **tundras** are very cold, flat habitats. They are found near the North Pole. They have frozen soil. They get very little rain. They have little diversity.

forest in fall

Analyze Which habitat has the most diversity? Put a check mark next to name of the land habitat. Tell why you think this habitat is the most diverse.

Science Practice
▸**Toolbox**

Plan an Investigation
How would you investigate which land habitat has the most diversity?

🌀 SC.2.N.1.1

tundra

desert

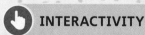

Grasslands

In the United States, grasslands are often called prairies. They are home to different types of grasses and bushes. Not many trees can grow. Grasslands can be cold or warm. Plants and animals that live in grasslands often have adaptations. For example, bison have woolly fur that help them stay warm.

Quest Connection

What are some plants and animals that live in a land habitat near you?

Habitat Diversity

Some habitats are more diverse than others. Diversity is one reason to protect many different habitats.

Look at the two habitats.

Identify Count the kinds of living things shown in each habitat. Write the number in the box.

Analyze Which habitat is more diverse? Why do you think it is more diverse?

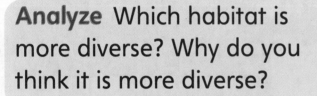

Living Things in Water Habitats

SC.2.L.17.2 Recognize and explain that living things are found all over Earth, but each is only able to live in habitats that meet its basic needs. (Also SC.2.N.1.1, SC.2.N.1.3, LAFS.2.RI.1.1, and LAFS.2.RI.1.2)

I can identify where plants and animals live in water.

Vocabulary

wetland

marsh

swamp

Jumpstart Discovery!

Circle an adaptation of a living thing in the picture. Tell why the adaptation helps the living thing survive in water.

How do plants survive in water?

Scientists make models of living things to study their adaptations. What adaptations help a plant live in water?

Design and Build

☐ 1. **Design a model** of a water plant. Draw and label your design. Show your design to your teacher.

☐ 2. Choose which materials you will use. Build and test your model.

Evaluate Your Design

3. What adaptations do plants need in a water habitat? How do you know?

_____

_____

_____

_____

Materials

• container with water

Suggested Materials

• clay
• gravel
• pipe cleaners
• paperclips
• cork pieces
• aluminum foil
• string
• craft sticks

Science Practice

Scientists design models to explain how things work.

The Ocean

The ocean is a large body of salt water. Some ocean habitats are warm. Others are cold. Some are icy.

Different plants and animals live in the ocean. Some live in the deep ocean. Others live near the surface. Others live near the shore.

▶ VIDEO

Watch a video on a coral reef habitat.

Visual Literacy

Look at the pictures. Explain what the ocean habitat provides for these living things.

Connecting Concepts ▸ Toolbox

Structure and Function

The bodies of whales are adapted to live in the ocean. Thick blubber keeps them warm. Large lungs help them dive deep. What are two other adaptations you can observe?

Rivers and Streams

Most rivers and streams are fresh water. Some rivers are wide and flow for hundreds of miles. Streams are smaller than rivers. Water in rivers and streams can flow quickly or slowly. Rivers and streams have a lot of diversity, including water plants and fish.

☑ Reading Check **Main Idea and Details** Circle the detail that compares the sizes of rivers and streams.

Quest Connection

Would you like to protect a water habitat or a land habitat? Explain your choice.

salmon swimming in a river

Wetlands

A **wetland** is a habitat that has both land and water. It can be covered with water all the time or just some of the time. The soil in a wetland is almost always wet. Wetlands have a lot of diversity. Many animals use wetlands to raise their young.

Marshes and swamps are wetlands. A **marsh** has plants that are like grasses. A **swamp** has plants that are like trees. Marshes and swamps may look like ponds during the wet season. During the dry season the soil stays wet.

Compare and Contrast Circle words that describe how a marsh and swamp are similar. Underline words that describe how they are different.

a swamp habitat

Why Some Animals Live in Water

Water habitats provide basic needs for animals that live there. These basic needs include water, shelter, and food.

Water habitats are diverse. Animals that live in water have certain features. These features help them survive in the habitat.

Identify Look at the pictures. Draw an X on the animal that does not belong to a water habitat. Tell why you think this animal does not belong. Tell why you think the other animals belong.

Infer Why do you think it is important to protect many different habitats?

QUEST CHECK ✓ OFF

MAFS.2.OA.1.1

Add and Subtract

A population is the number of living things in a habitat. Populations change over time. Scientists use math. They calculate the size of a population.

There were 60 dolphins in a habitat. In one year, 32 dolphin calves were born, 7 dolphins died, and 10 moved to a new habitat.

Calculate How many dolphins are in the population now?

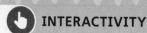

Protect a Habitat

Why protect a local habitat?

Think of all the land and water habitats you learned about. How does a habitat support living things? Why is it important to protect a habitat? Now it is time to choose a habitat to protect.

Show What You Know

Share information about the habitat you chose. Be creative! For example, you could make a video, a poster, or a slideshow. Remember to include important features of the habitat. Explain why the habitat is important. Tell which resources it has. Identify which living things need that habitat.

Career Connection

Ecologist

Ecologists study living things and their habitats. They work to protect habitats. Some ecologists travel all over the world. Others work in a laboratory.

Ecologists want to know how living and nonliving things interact. They also want to know how living things use their habitats.

These scientists communicate their research to governments and to other scientists. They suggest ways to protect different habitats.

Would you like to be an ecologist? Why or why not?

_____

_____

_____

_____

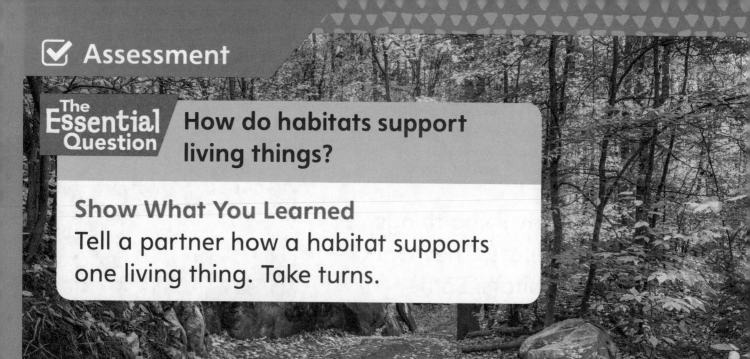

The Essential Question How do habitats support living things?

Show What You Learned
Tell a partner how a habitat supports one living thing. Take turns.

Read each question and choose or write the best answer.

1. Label each habitat. Identify one feature of each habitat.

2. Describe how the diversity in a forest habitat is different than the diversity in a desert habitat.

_____

_____

_____

_____

3. Draw a line between the living thing and its habitat.

river

desert

forest

4. Sometimes people build houses on land that used to be a wetland habitat. How might building houses in this habitat impact the environment?

   a. It might flood.

   b. It might be very icy.

   c. It might have salt water.

   d. It might be too dry.

Read the scenario and answer questions 1–2.

Henry drew a model of a habitat in Africa.

1 Which two kinds of habitats is the model habitat most similar to?
- Ⓐ tundra and wetland
- Ⓑ grassland and forest
- Ⓒ desert and tundra
- Ⓓ forest and marsh

2 Do you think this habitat needs a lot of water?
- Ⓕ Yes, because there are many large animals.
- Ⓖ Yes, because it looks like it is very large.
- Ⓗ No, because large animals can store water.
- Ⓘ No, because there are not many trees.

Read the scenario and answer questions 3–4.

Martha read about and recorded living things found in different habitats.

Habitat	Living Things
river	frogs, fish, cattails, water fleas
wetland	ducks, beavers, mosquitoes
forest	snakes, birds, oak trees, ants
desert	cacti, grass, bobcats, beetles

3 Which habitats support similar kinds of living things?
- Ⓐ river and forest
- Ⓑ river and wetland
- Ⓒ wetland and desert
- Ⓓ river and desert

4 Which kind of animal could **best** survive in all four of the habitats?
- Ⓕ insects
- Ⓖ fish
- Ⓗ mammals
- Ⓘ birds

How can you compare diversity in two habitats?

Scientists learn about habitats by observing them. How can you observe habitats to compare their diversity?

Suggested Materials

- hand lens
- collecting jar
- ruler

Procedure

☐ 1. As a class you will **observe** two habitats near you. How can you observe the habitats? What materials will you use?

Science Practice

Scientists make observations to understand details about something.

_____

_____

_____

_____

☐ 2. **Observe** the habitats. **Collect data** on living and nonliving things.

Observations

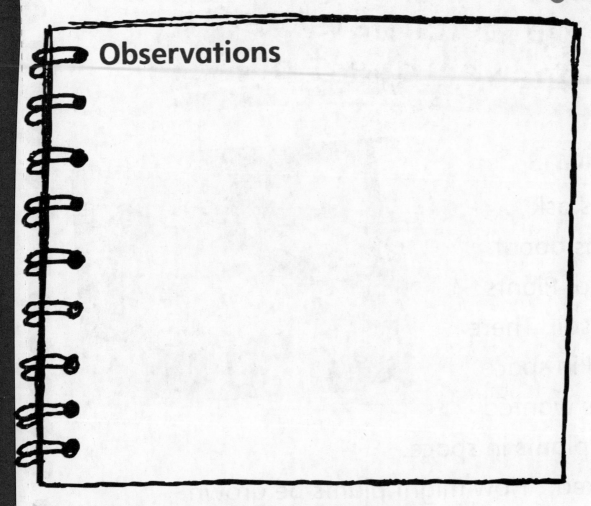

Analyze and Interpret Data

3. **Use Evidence** Based on your data, tell which habitat has more living things.

4. **Infer** Why do you think one habitat has more living things than the other?

_____

- -

_____

_____

- -

_____

How do scientists ask and answer questions?

Questions

Scientists ask questions about the world. Plants grow in soil. There is no soil in space. Scientists wanted to grow plants in space. They asked, "How might plants be grown without soil?"

Underline a question that scientists asked. Write a question you might ask about plants in space.

_____

_____

_____

_____

SC.2.N.1.1 Raise questions about the natural world, investigate them in teams through free exploration and systematic observations, and generate appropriate explanations based on those explorations.

Investigations

You investigate to look for answers. Scientists investigated ways to grow plants without soil. Plants need nutrients from soil. Scientists added nutrients to water. They put the roots of some plants in the water. They observed how the plants grew.

Scientists shared what they learned. They explained how plants could grow in space without soil.

Circle what scientists investigated.

Underline how scientists investigated.

How do scientists make observations?

Your Senses

Scientists use their senses to observe the world. They can look, hear, smell, touch and taste. Then, they can tell others what they observed.

Tell which sense each scientist is using.

Tools

Scientists observe in many ways. Sometimes they use tools to observe. Scientists can use a thermometer to tell how warm something is. They use other tools to see small things better.

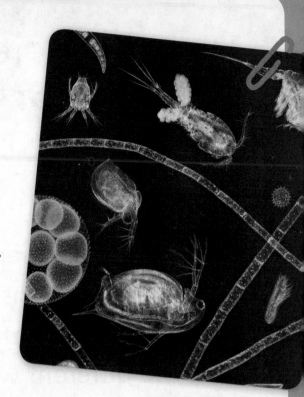

This scientist is looking at a drop of water with a microscope. How does the microscope help her?

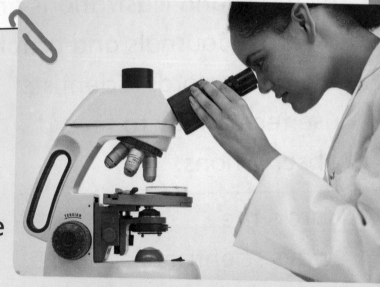

_____

_____

_____

_____

How do scientists keep records?

Records

Scientists make observations during investigations. They record their observations. There are different ways to keep records. Charts, pictures, and illustrations are records. Journals and graphs are also records. Scientists use technology to record observations.

Circle the ways scientists can record observations.

Observations

Scientists make observations when they investigate. They share what they observe with other scientists. Other scientists do the investigation in the same way. Then, the groups of scientists can compare their observations. They find out if they got similar results.

Why should these scientists compare their observations?

_____

_____

_____

_____

How do scientists know if their results can be trusted?

Evidence

Scientists want their work to be trusted.
They use evidence in their work.
Evidence is a set of observations that
shows something is most likely true.

parakeets

The picture shows blue parakeets. A student states that parakeets can be different colors. How can he prove his statement with evidence?

_____

_____

_____

_____

SC.2.N.1.3 Ask "how do you know?" in appropriate situations and attempt reasonable answers when asked the same question by others.

SC.2.N.1.5 Distinguish between empirical observation (what you see, hear, feel, smell, or taste) and ideas or inferences (what you think).

Inferences

Scientists use their evidence to make inferences. Inferences are conclusions about an investigation.

In an investigation, scientists ask questions. They gather and record observations and evidence. Then, they make inferences to answer their questions.

A scientist studies bean plants. She gives one plant water and the other plant orange juice. She measures the height of each plant each day. She records her observations in the chart. What inference can the scientist make?

	Day 1	Day 3	Day 5
Water	10 cm	13 cm	17 cm
Orange juice	11 cm	8 cm	5 cm

Why do scientists repeat investigations?

Repeat Investigations

Scientists can make mistakes. A scientist might record a temperature incorrectly. This can lead to incorrect conclusions. Scientists may choose to do the same investigation, in the same way, many times. This helps scientists check their results. If they get the same result each time, then it is more likely their conclusions are true.

Underline why scientists repeat their investigations.

SC.2.N.1.4 Explain how particular scientific investigations should yield similar conclusions when repeated.

SC.2.N.1.6 Explain how scientists alone or in groups are always investigating new ways to solve problems.

Groups at Work

Scientists often work in groups. Working in groups helps them share ideas. It helps them answer questions. Working in groups helps the scientists look at their work differently.

When scientists work together they can learn from each other. When scientists share what they know, they can figure out many different ways to solve problems.

Would you rather work with others or alone? Explain why.

Glossary

The glossary uses letters and signs to show how words are pronounced. The mark ′ is placed after a syllable with a primary or heavy accent. The mark ′ is placed after a syllable with a secondary or lighter accent.

A

adaptation (ad′ ap tā′ shən) A characteristic of a living thing that helps it survive in its habitat. The thorns on a rose stem are an **adaptation**.

animal (an′ ə məl) A living thing that cannot make its own food. A dog is an **animal**.

assemble (ə sem′ bəl) To put something together. You can **assemble** a puzzle by fitting its pieces together.

attract (ə trakt′) To pull toward something. A magnet can **attract** some metal objects but not others.

brain (brān) The body part that controls everything the body does. Your **brain** tells you how far to jump when playing hopscotch.

clay (klā) Soil made of small pieces of rock packed together. The sticky soil near the river was mostly **clay**.

diversity (də vėr′ sə tē) The different kinds of plants and animals in one place. Rainforests have a lot of **diversity**.

electricity (i lek′ tris′ ə tē) A kind of energy that moves through wires and can make light and heat. A lamp uses **electricity** to light your room.

energy (en′ ər jē) The ability to do work or cause change. **Energy** from the sun makes summer days warm.

evaporation (i vap′ ə rā′ shən) The process of changing a liquid into a gas. The water on the sidewalk disappeared through **evaporation**.

flexibility (flek′ sə bil′ ə tē) The ability of matter to bend. Rubber has more **flexibility** than metal.

force (fôrs) A push or a pull that makes something move. He used **force** to swing the bat and hit the ball.

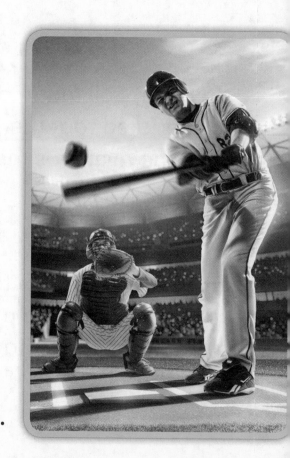

gas (gas) Matter that does not have its own shape or size. Hot **gas** inside the balloon made it rise into the sky.

gravity (grav′ ə tē) A force that pulls objects toward the center of Earth. The ball falls to the ground because of **gravity**.

habitat (hab′ ə tat) A place where a plant or animal lives. A rain forest is a kind of land **habitat**.

hardness (härd′ nes) How hard or solid an object is compared to other objects. A diamond has greater **hardness** than any other material.

heart (härt) The muscle that pumps blood through the body. Your **heart** is about the size of your fist.

humus (hyü′ məs) Soil material that is a mix of nutrients from small pieces of dead plants and animals. Adding **humus** to your garden will help your plants grow.

hurricane (hėr′ ə kān) A large storm that starts over warm ocean water. The **hurricane** snapped many trees and caused flooding.

kinetic energy (kin net′ ik en′ ər jē) The energy of motion. A jumping cat has a lot of **kinetic energy**.

life cycle (līf′ sī′ kəl) The way living things grow and change. A seed is part of the **life cycle** of an apple tree.

liquid (lik′ wid) Matter that does not have its own shape. He poured the **liquid** into the glass.

loam (lōm) Soil that is made of sand, clay, silt, and humus. Most of the soil in my garden is **loam**.

lung (lung) A body part that helps some animals breathe air. He took a deep breath to fill his **lungs** with air.

magnet (mag′ nit) Something that can push or pull some metal objects. He used a **magnet** to pick up the paper clips.

magnetic (mag net′ ik) An object that can be pushed or pulled by a magnet. Some types of metals are **magnetic**.

marsh (märsh) A wetland with plants that are mostly like grasses. Many ducks live in the **marsh** near my house.

matter (mat′ ər) Anything that has weight and takes up space. Solids, liquids, and gases are forms of **matter**.

mineral (min′ ər əl) Nonliving material that comes from Earth. Most rocks are made of more than one **mineral.**

motion (mō′ shən) What happens when an object moves. The bouncing **motion** of the toy made us laugh.

muscle (mus′əl) A body part that helps animals move. You use **muscles** in your legs to walk.

nutrient (nü′ trē ənt) A material that helps living things grow. Fruits and vegetables have many important **nutrients.**

pattern (pat′ ərn) Something that repeats. The stripes on the caterpillar form a pretty **pattern.**

plant (plant) A living thing that can use energy from the sun to make its own food. Trees and grasses are different kinds of **plants**.

pollution (pə lü′ shən) A material in air, water, or land that can cause harm. Trash in the river is a kind of **pollution**.

potential energy (pə ten′ shəl en′ ər jē) Stored energy related to an object's position. A rock on the edge of a cliff has a lot of **potential energy**.

precipitation (pri cip′ ə tā′ shən) Water that falls from the sky to Earth. The weather report said we would get heavy **precipitation**.

property (prop′ ər tē) A trait or feature of an object. Color is a **property** of minerals.

Glossary

purpose (pėr′ pəs) The use of an object. The **purpose** of using a ruler is to help draw a straight line.

repel (ri pel′) To push away from something. The waxy surface of the box helped **repel** water.

reversible (ri vėr′ sə bəl) To change something back to the way it was. Melting ice is a **reversible** change.

rock (rok) A hard, solid part of Earth. The surface of Earth is made up of **rock** under a layer of soil.

season (sē′ zn) One of the four parts of the year with a different weather pattern. It usually snows during the winter **season** where I live.

severe weather (sə vir′ weᴛʜ′ ər) Weather that is dangerous. The dark clouds and strong winds meant that **severe weather** was coming.

shelter (shel′ tər) A place that protects animals. The barn provides **shelter** for the farm animals.

skeleton (skel′ ə tən) The bones that hold the body together. She knows the name of every bone in the **skeleton**.

solid (sol′ id) Matter that has its own size and shape. Ice is the **solid** form of water.

speed (spēd) How fast or slow an object is moving. Cars move with a lot of **speed** during a race.

state (stāt) A form of matter. Water changes **state** when it freezes into ice.

stomach (stum′ ək) A body part that helps break down food into nutrients. My **stomach** makes noises when I am hungry.

swamp (swämp) A wetland with plants that are mostly trees. The water is deep in some parts of the **swamp**.

temperature (tem′ pər ə chər) How hot or cold something is. The air **temperature** is usually lower in fall than in summer.

texture (teks′ chər) How something feels. Ice cream has a smooth **texture**.

thunderstorm (thun′ dər stôrm′) Weather with thunder, lightning, strong winds, and heavy rain. We ran home when the **thunderstorm** started.

tornado (tôr nā′ dō) A column of wind shaped like a funnel. A **tornado** sometimes happens during a thunderstorm.

tundra (tun′ drə) A very cold, flat habitat near the North Pole. The **tundra** soil remains frozen even in the summer.

water cycle (wȯt′ ər sī′ kəl) The pattern of water moving from Earth's surface to the air and back again. Rain and snow return water to Earth's surface through the **water cycle**.

water vapor (wȯt′ ər vā′ pər) The gas form of water. You cannot see **water vapor** but you can feel it on a muggy day.

weight (wāt) How heavy an object is. The **weight** of the box made it too heavy to carry.

wetland (wet′ land′) A land habitat that is often covered with water. Marshes and swamps are two kinds of **wetlands.**

wind (wind) Air that is moving. The leaves moved gently in the summer **wind.**

Index

Index

Index

Index

Index

Index

Index

Credits

Illustrations

Peter Bull Art Studio; Sara Lynn Cramb/Astound US; Peter Francis/MB Artists, Inc.; Lauren Gallegos/C.A. Tugeau, LLC; Patrick Gnan/IllustrationOnline.com; Bob Kayganich/IllustrationOnline.com; Kristen Kest/MB Artists, Inc.; Erika LeBarre/IllustrationOnline.com; Matt LeBarre/Blasco Creative, LLC; Lisa Manuzak/Astound; Precision Graphics/Lachina Publishing Services; Geoffrey P Smith; Jamie Smith/MB Artists, Inc.; Mark Rogalski/Painted Words, Inc.; Mike Rothman/Melissa Turk; Ralph Voltz/IllustrationOnline.com

Photographs

Photo locators denoted as follows: Top (T), Center (C), Bottom (B), Left (L), Right (R), Background (Bkgd)

Front Cover: Brunner Sébastien/LazyPixel/Getty Images;
Back Cover: Marinello/DigitalVision Vectors/Getty Images

FM

iv: Tanarch/Shutterstock; vi: Budimir Jevtic/Fotolia; vii: Michael Jung/Fotolia; viii:Dragon Images/Shutterstock; ix: Asier Romero/Shutterstock; x: Wavebreakmedia/Shutterstock; xi: Noel Hendrickson/Getty Images; xii Bkgrd: Brian J. Skerry/National Geographic/Getty Images; xii TR: Old Apple/Shutterstock

T01

1: Liseykina/Shutterstock; 2 CR: Simon Tang/Fotolia; 2 TR: Budimir Jevtic/Fotolia; 5 Bkgrd: Vladimir Dokovski/Shutterstock; 5 CR: Yands/iStock/Getty Images; 6: Photocay/Alamy Stock Photo; 7: Sergei Telegin/Shutterstock; 8 Bkgrd: Siimsepp/Fotolia; 8 CR: Woe/Fotolia; 8 TR: Sabena Jane Blackbird/Alamy Stock Photo; 9 BR: Budimir Jevtic/Fotolia; 9 C: Tyler Boyes/Fotolia; 9 CL: Aleksandr Pobedimskiy/Shutterstock; 9 CR: Kletr/Shutterstock; 10 B: Vvoe/Shutterstock; 10 CR: Jeffrey Daly/Fotolia; 10 TC: 123RF; 11 Bkgrd: Tashatuvango/Shutterstock; 11 C: Bob Gibbons/Alamy Stock Photo; 11 TL: Budimir Jevtic/Fotolia; 12: Ivonne Wierink/Fotolia; 13: Jiang Hongyan/Shutterstock; 14: John D. Williams/Fotolia; 15 BC: Timothy Hearsum/AGE Fotostock; 15 BL: Greg Wright/Alamy Stock Photo; 15 BR: Doug McCutcheon/Alamy Stock Photo; 16 BC: Budimir Jevtic/Fotolia; 16 BR: Topic Photo Agency/AGE Fotostock; 17 BC: Greg Wright/Alamy Stock Photo; 17 BL: Doug McCutcheon/Alamy Stock Photo; 17 BR: Timothy Hearsum/AGE Fotostock; 17 C: 123RF; 17 CL: Zeljko Radojko/Shutterstock; 17 CR: Denis and Yulia Pogostins/Shutterstock; 17 TL: Budimir Jevtic/Fotolia; 18: Hcast/Fotolia; 19: Bouvier Sandrine/123RF; 22 T: Travnikov Studio/Shutterstock; 22 TR: TerryM/Shutterstock; 23 BC: Budimir Jevtic/Fotolia; 23 Bkgrd: Phaitoon Sutunyawatcha/Shutterstock; 23 CR: Family Business/Fotolia; 23 TR : Manfredxy/Shutterstock; 24 Bkgrd: Tristan/Fotolia; 24 CR: Jonbilous/Fotolia; 24 TR: Dhoxax/Shutterstock; 25 BL: Jerry Lin/Shutterstock; 25 BR: David Lade/Shutterstock; 25 CL: Marie C Fields/Shutterstock; 25 CR: Vlad Siaber/Shutterstock; 25 TL: Budimir Jevtic/Fotolia; 28 Bkgrd: Iakov Kalinin/Shutterstock; 28 C: Budimir Jevtic/Fotolia; 30: Kushnirov Avraham/Fotolia; 32: Budimir Jevtic/Fotolia; 33: Yuriy Kulik/Shutterstock; 34: Imagevixen/Getty Images; 36: Photosquirrel/Fotolia; 37 BR: Budimir Jevtic/Fotolia; 37 CR: Joel_420/Shutterstock; 37 TR: Pixfly/Shutterstock; 38 B: Jon Manjeot/Shutterstock; 38 TL: Budimir Jevtic/Fotolia; 39 B: Raymond Gehman/Getty Images; 39 TR: National Oceanic and Atmospheric Administration/Department of Commerce.; 40: The Perfect Moment/Fotolia; 41: James Threw/Fotolia; 42: Vchal/Shutterstock; 43 Bkgrd: playalife2006/123RF; 43 BR: Budimir Jevtic/Fotolia; 44 C: Budimir Jevtic/Fotolia; 44 CL: Matthijs Wetterauw/Alamy; 46 Bkgrd: Simon Tang/Fotolia; 46 CR: Budimir Jevtic/Fotolia; 46 T: Stevegeer/iStock/Getty Images; 47 Bkgrd: Fedorov Oleksiy./Shutterstock; 47 TR: Wayne Hutchinson/Alamy Stock Photo; 48: Blickwinke /Alamy Stock Photo; 49: Fonta83/Fotolia; 53: Serg64/Shutterstock; Kindersley Ltd/Alamy Stock Photo;

T02

54: Avalon_Studio/Getty Images; 56: Michael Jung/Fotolia; 58: Roxana Bashyrova/Shutterstock; 59 B: Photosync/Fotolia; 59 C: Vlad Ivantcov/Fotolia; 61: Richard Peterson/Shutterstock; 62 Bkgrd: Andreas von Einsiedel/Alamy Stock Photo; 62 TR: Elenathewise/Fotolia; 63 R: Chones/Fotolia; 64 BC: Michael Jung/Fotolia; 64 R: Smneedham/Getty Images; 65 TC: Valerii Zan/Fotolia; 65 TCL: Pukach/Shutterstock; 65 TCR: Monticello/Shutterstock; 65 TL: Michael Jung/Fotolia; 66 BL: Robert McGouey/Wildlife /Alamy Stock Photo; 66 BR: Vladimir Wrangel/Fotolia; 67: Diana Taliun/Fotolia; 68: Leon Werdinger/Alamy Stock Photo; 69: Robert McGouey/Wildlife /Alamy Stock Photo; 70 Bkgrd: Ivoha/Shutterstock; 70 TCR: Artem Shadrin/Shutterstock; 72 BR: Michael Jung/Fotolia; 72 CR: Dorling Kindersley Ltd/Alamy Stock Photo; 72 TR: Photonic 11/Alamy Stock Photo; 73 C: Dmitriy/Fotolia; 73 TL: Michael Jung/Fotolia; 74: Africa Studio/Shutterstock; 77: Michael Jung/Fotolia; 78: Michael Jung/Fotolia; 81: Ilya Akinshin/Fotolia; 82 BC: Michael Jung/Fotolia; 82 CR: Tim Ridley/Dorling Kindersley, Ltd.; 82 TR: Nikita Rogul/Shutterstock; 83 CL: Arina P Habich/Shutterstock; 83 R: Michelle McMahon/Getty Images; 85 CR: James A. Harris/Shutterstock; 85 TR: Itsik Marom/Alamy Stock Photo; 86 B: Ann Baldwin/Shutterstock; 86 TL: Michael Jung/Fotolia; 87 B: 123rf.com; 87 BL: Natali Glado/Shutterstock; 87 BR: Iakov Kalinin/Shutterstock; 87 CR: Artazum/Shutterstock; 87 CR: Nikkytok/Shutterstock; 88 BC: Michael Jung/Fotolia; 88 Bkgrd: Justin Yeung/Alamy Stock Photo; 89 Bkgrd: Andy Crawford/Dorling Kindersley, Ltd.; 89 TR: Blue Jean Images/Alamy Stock Photo; 90 BR: Aaron Amat/Shutterstock; 90 T: Donatas1205/Shutterstock; 91: Tim Large/Alamy Stock Photo; 94: Lina Balciunaite/Shutterstock

T03

96: Paul Souders/Digital Vision/Getty Images; 98: Dragon Images/Shutterstock; 100: OnlyZoia/Shutterstock; 101 Bkgrd: Tankist276/Shutterstock; 101 CR: Pixelbliss/Shutterstock; 102: Digital Vision/Getty Images; 104: Dragon Images/Shutterstock; 105: WoodenDinosaur/Getty Images; 106 B: Apiguide/Shutterstock; 106 TR: Sergey Peterman/Shutterstock; 107 BR: Viktor1/Shutterstock; 107 CL: Lydia Vero/Shutterstock; 107 CR: NA HNWD/Shutterstock; 107 TL: Dragon Images/Shutterstock; 107 TR: Cherezoff/Shutterstock; 108: Independent Picture Service/UIG/Getty Images; 110 Bkgrd: Vikki Hunt/Alamy Stock Photo; 110 CL: Florida Stock/Shutterstock; 111: Dragon Images/Shutterstock; 112 BL: Science Photo/Shutterstock; 112 BR: Valentyn Volk

Shutterstock; 112 CL: Peangdao/Shutterstock; 112 CR: Ed Samuel/Shutterstock; 113 CR: Yueh Hung Shih/Alamy Stock Photo; 113 TL: Dragon Images/Shutterstock; 114: Christoffer Vika/Fotolia; 117: Dragon Images/Shutterstock; 118 BR: Peter Titmuss/Alamy Stock Photo; 118 TC: Dragon Images/Shutterstock; 119 BR: Ersin Ergin/Shutterstock; 119 TR: ChameleonsEye/Shutterstock; 120: John Muggenborg/Alamy Stock Photo; 122 Bkgrd: Geoff Brightling/Tharp Modelmakers/Dorling Kindersley; 122 C: Dragon Images/Shutterstock; 123 Bkgrd: ilkercelik/Shutterstock; 123 TR: Peter Close/Shutterstock; 124: Sheff/Shutterstock; 128: John Kasawa/Shutterstock; John Kasawa/Shutterstock

T04

130: Eugene Onischenko/Shutterstock; 132: Asier Romero/Shutterstock; 135: Aerovista Luchtfotografie/Shutterstock; 136: Guynamedjames/Alamy Stock Photo; 138: Dušan Zidar/Alamy Stock Photo; 139 CR: Justin Kase zsixz/Alamy Stock Photo; 139 TR: Konstantin Sutyagin/Shutterstock; 140 BC: Asier Romero/Shutterstock; 140 Bkgrd: Ian Ward/The National Trust Photolibrary/Alamy Stock Photo; 140 CR: Martin Kemp/Shutterstock; 141 CL: Lois McCleary/Getty Images; 141 CR: Alexey Maximenko/123RF; 141 TL: Asier Romero/Shutterstock; 144 Bkgrd: Leonid Andronov/Fotolia; 144 CR: Phildaint/Shutterstock; 145 CR: Tatiana Popova/Shutterstock; 145 TR: Tatiana Popova/Shutterstock; 146 Bkgrd: Photographee.eu/Shutterstock; 147 CL: INSADCO Photography/Alamy Stock Photo; 147 CR: Damon Yancy/Shutterstock; 147 TL: Asier Romero/Shutterstock; 148 BR: Asier Romero/Shutterstock; 148: 103tnn/Fotolia; 150 Bkgrd: Inti St Clair/Getty Images; 150 TR: Fotokostic/Shutterstock; 151 BC: Asier Romero/Shutterstock; 151 TR: Jorg Hackemann/Shutterstcok; 152: bikeriderlondon/Shutterstock; 153 CL: Tyler Olsen/Fotolia; 153 CR: Sam Edwards/Getty Images; 153 TL: Asier Romero/Shutterstock; 154: Jeremy Walker/Science Photo Library/Getty Images; 155: Sergio Delle Vedove/Shutterstock; 157: Asier Romero/Shutterstock; 158 R: Zargon Design/Getty Images; 158 TL: Asier Romero/Shutterstock; 159 BR: Cylonphoto/Fotolia; 159 TR: Pippee29/Fotolia; 162 Bkgrd: Alexei Tm/Alamy Stock Photo; 162 CL: Mark Herreid/Shutterstock; 162 CR: Zelenskaya/Shutterstock; 164 B: Sarah Cheriton Jones/Shutterstock; 164 BL: Juniors Bildarchiv GmbH/Alamy Stock Photo; 164 TR: Hans Zaglitsch/ImageBROKER/Alamy Stock Photo; 165 BR: Asier Romero/Shutterstock; 165 T: Pal Teravagimov/Shutterstock; 166 BR: Nicha/Shutterstock; 166 TR: Asier Romero/Shutterstock; 168: Stephen Denness/Shutterstock; 170 Bkgrd: Michael Conde/EyeEm/Getty Images; 170 BR: Asier Romero/Shutterstock; 171 Bkgrd: Luciano Mortula/Shutterstock; 171 TR: Shestakoff/Shutterstock; 172: Devy/Shutterstock; 173: Juniors Bildarchiv GmbH/Alamy Stock Photo; 176: John Green/Cal Sport Media/Alamy Stock Photo; DELETE: Beata Aldridge/123RF

T05

178: Yuen Man Cheung/Alamy Stock Photo; 180: Wavebreakmedia/Shutterstock; 182: tanuha2001/Shutterstock; 183: Design Pics Inc/Alamy Stock Photo; 185 BR: Sumstock/Fotolia; 185 CR: domnitsky/Fotolia; 186 Bkgrd: Claire Higgins/Getty Images; 186 BR: Wavebreakmedia/Shutterstock; 187 BC: MarkGillow/Getty Images; 187 BC: Sofiaworld/Shutterstock; 187 L: Marie C Fields/Shutterstock; 187 R: Jean Faucett/Shutterstock;

188 BR: Will & Deni McIntyre/Science Source; 188 TR: Ron Rowan Photography/Shutterstock; 189 B: rruntsch/Fotolia; 189 TC: Rafael Ben Ari /Shutterstock; 190 BCR: DP Wildlife Vertebrates/Alamy Stock Photo; 190 BR: Vitalii Hulai/Fotolia; 190 C: Angelique van Heertum/Shutterstock; 190 CR: Avalon/Photoshot License/Alamy Stock Photo; 190 TR: Corey Ford/Alamy Stock Photo; 191 BC: brianguest/Fotolia; 191 BL: Peter Jordan_NE/Alamy Stock Photo; 191 BR: Serg64/Shutterstock; 191 C: xelena/Shutterstock; 191 CL: Siede Preis/Getty Images; 191 CR: Irina Kryvasheina/Alamy Stock Photo; 191 TL: Wavebreakmedia/Shutterstock; 192: Fotokostic/Shutterstock; 193: Darla Krav/Shutterstock; 195 BR: Wavebreakmedia/Shutterstock; 195 CR: Olesia Bilkei/Shutterstock; 195 TR: Filipe B. Varela/Shutterstock; 196 BR: Ines Behrens Kunkel/Shutterstock; 196 TC: Wavebreakmedia/Shutterstock; 198: Toby Houlton/Alamy Stock Photo; 200: Wavebreakmedia/Shutterstock; 201: hkuchera/Fotolia; 202 BL: photomatz/Shutterstock; 202 BR: Valeniker/Shutterstock; 202 CL: Chamnan Phanthong/Fotolia; 202 TL: Wavebreakmedia/Shutterstock; 202 TR: 35level53/Fotolia; 203 B: Dennis W Donohue/Shutterstock; 203 TR: RTimages/Alamy Stock Photo; 204: FatCamera/Getty Images; 206: Wavebreakmedia/Shutterstock; 207: Sergey Novikov/Shutterstock; 208: Anna Bizon/Getty Images; 209 Bkgrd: travelibUK/Alamy Stock Photo; 209 TL: Wavebreakmedia/Shutterstock; 210 B: Javier Brosch/Shutterstock; 210 TR: Chris Willson/Alamy Stock Photo; 212 Bkgrd: Alexandra Radu/Alamy Stock Photo; 212 BR: Wavebreakmedia/Shutterstock; 213 Bkgrd: photoinnovation/Shutterstock; 213 TR: Colin Anderson/Getty Images; 214: Sergii Figurnyi/Fotolia; 217 C: owatta/Shutterstock; 217 CR: Mureu/Shutterstock; 218: Martin Shields/Alamy Stock Photo; Martin Shields/Alamy Stock Photo

T06

220: Ondrej Prosicky/Shutterstock; 222: Noel Hendrickson/Getty Images; 225: Jones/Shimlock Secret Sea Visions/Getty Images; 226: Joe Mamer Photography/Alamy Stock Photo; 228: Georgette Douwma/Getty Images; 229: Noel Hendrickson/Getty Images; 230: Noel Hendrickson/Getty Images; 231 BL: Clinton Weaver/123 RF; 231 BR: svf74/Fotolia; 232: Druvo/Getty Images; 233: JPL/NASA; 236: Joyfnp/Getty Images; 237 L: Arildina/Shutterstock; 237 R: Richard Garvey Williams/Alamy Stock Photo; 238 BC: Noel Hendrickson/Getty Images; 238 Bkgrd: Philippe Widling/AGE Fotostock; 239 BR: LMspencer/Shutterstock; 239 TL: Noel Hendrickson/Getty Images; 239 TR: Kwest/Shutterstock; 240: Joost van Uffelen/Shutterstock; 242 B: Isabelle Kuehn/Shutterstock; 242 TR: Gudkov Andrey/Shutterstock; 243 BL: Rich Carey/Shutterstock; 243 R: Bashiri/Fotolia; 244 Bkgrd: Beat J. Korner/Shutterstock; 244 C: Noel Hendrickson/Getty Images; 245: John Dreyer/Getty Images; 246 BCR: Predrag Lukic/Shutterstock; 246 Bkgrd: Yuriy Kulik/Shutterstock; 246 BR: Life On White/Getty Images; 246 CR: Frantisek Czanner/Shutterstock; 246 TL: Noel Hendrickson/Getty Images; 246 TR: OneSmallSquare/Shutterstock; 247: Alexander Chaikin/Shutterstock; 248 Bkgrd: youngvet/Getty Images; 248 C: Noel Hendrickson/Getty Images; 248 T: Butterfly Hunter/Shutterstock; 249 Bkgrd: Hero Images/Getty Images; 249 T: Liliboas/Getty Images; 249 TR: FangXiaNuo/Getty Images; 250 BL:

My Notes and Designs

Draw, Write, Create

My Notes and Designs

Draw, Write, Create

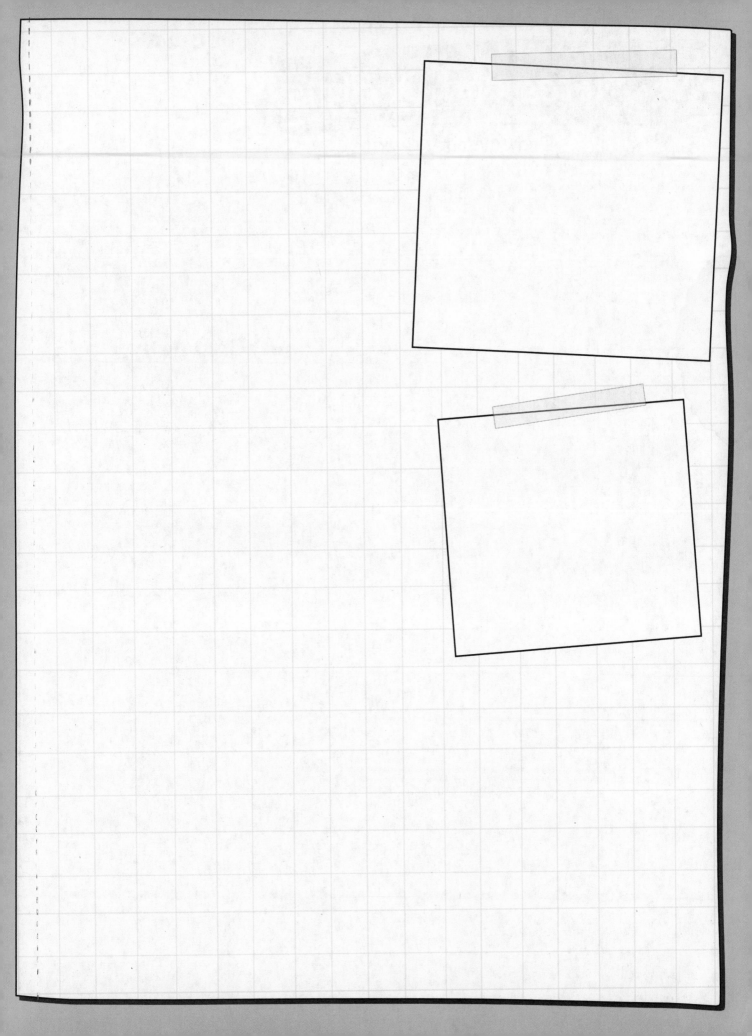

My Notes and Designs

Draw, Write, Create

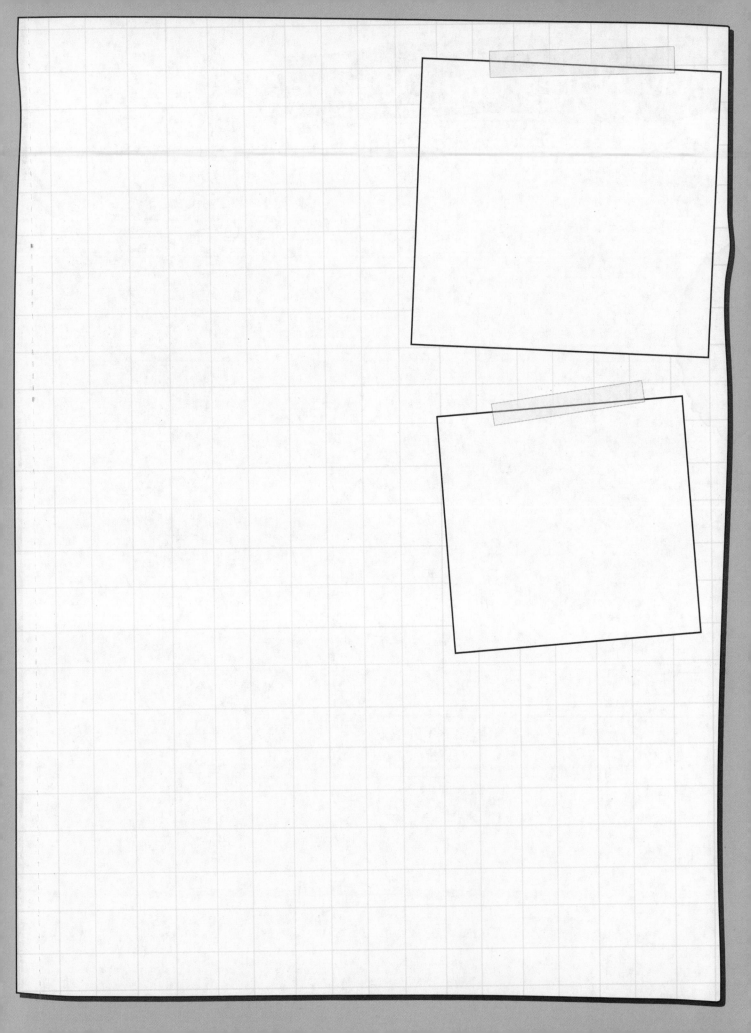

My Notes and Designs

Draw, Write, Create

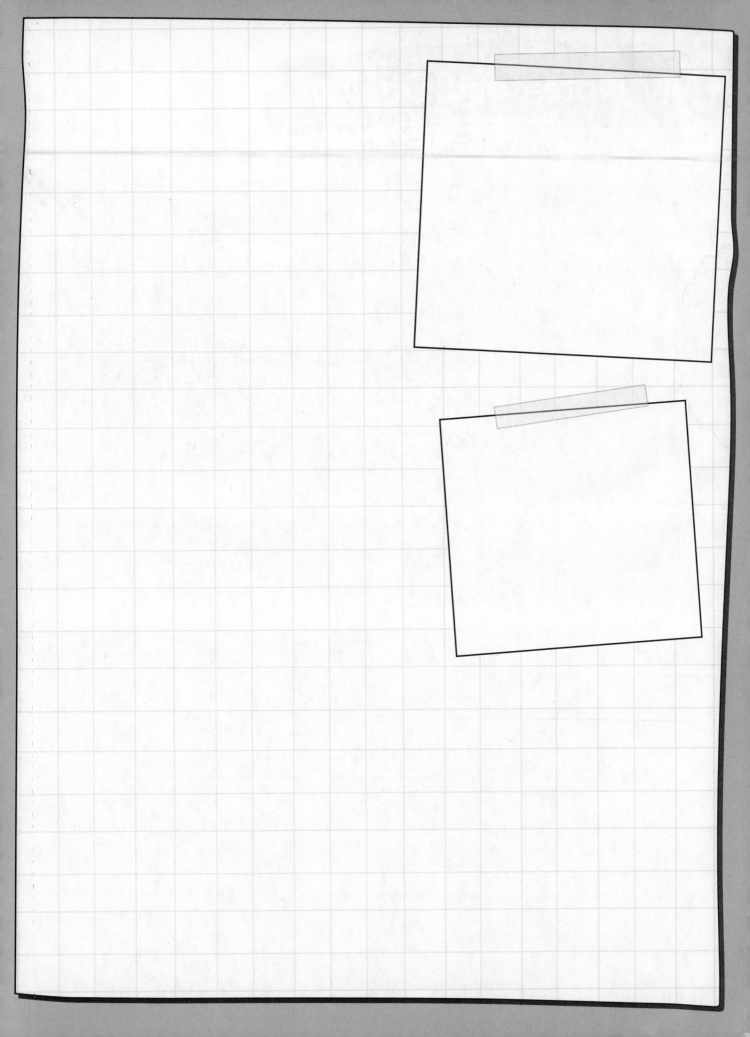

My Notes and Designs

Draw, Write, Create

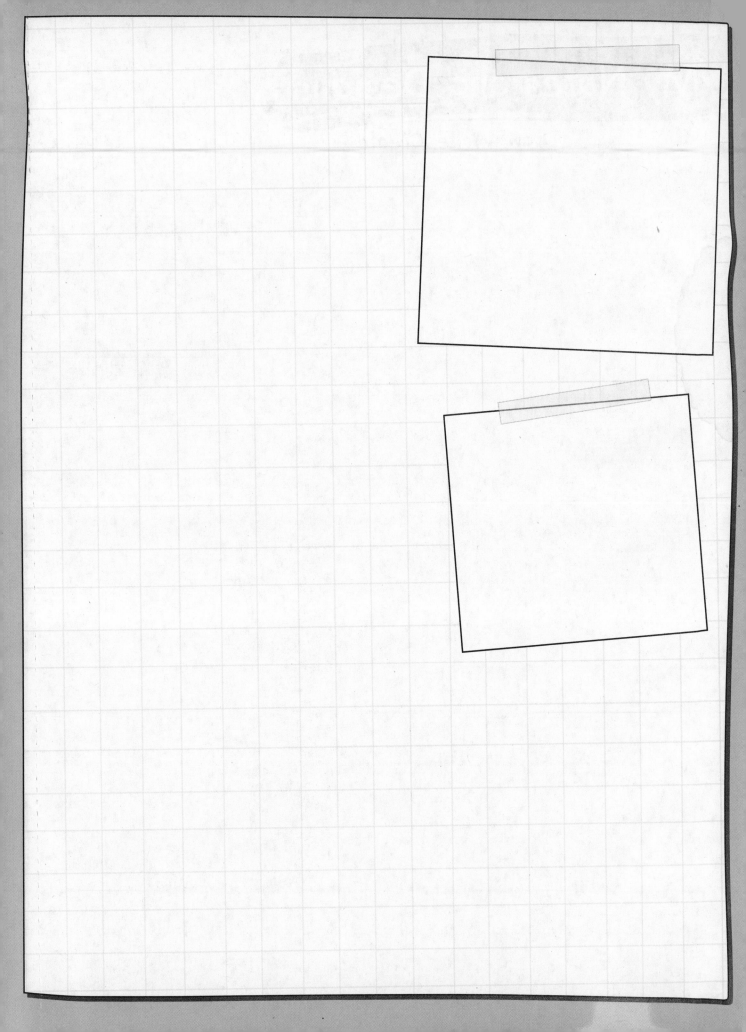

My Notes and Designs

Draw, Write, Create